The Myths of Security

What the Computer Security Industry
Doesn't Want You to Know

The Myths of Security

What the Computer Security Industry
Doesn't Want You to Know

John Viega

O'REILLY®

Beijing • Cambridge • Farnham • Köln • Sebastopol • Taipei • Tokyo

The Myths of Security: What the Computer Security Industry Doesn't Want You to Know
by John Viega

Published by O'Reilly Media, Inc., 1005 Gravenstein Highway North,
Sebastopol, CA 95472.

O'Reilly books may be purchased for educational, business, or sales promotional
use. Online editions are also available for most titles (*my.safaribooksonline.com*).
For more information, contact our corporate/institutional sales department:
(800) 998-9938 or *corporate@oreilly.com*.

Editor: Mike Loukides

Production Editor:
    Rachel Monaghan

Copyeditor: Amy Thomson

Proofreader: Rachel Monaghan

Indexer: Angela Howard

Cover Designer: Mark Paglietti

Interior Designer: Ron Bilodeau

Illustrator: Robert Romano

Printing History:

June 2009:   First Edition.

ISBN: 978-0-596-52302-2

[M]

Contents

Foreword

Everybody with a computer should worry a little about whether hackers might break in and steal personal data. After all, software is complex and has lots of flaws—and people can be tricked by a good ruse. People are in over their heads in trying to figure out this difficult problem, and they need a good security product that works, is easy to use, and doesn't impact the performance of their machines.

The security industry should be coming to the rescue. But in this book, John Viega shows why many people are at risk when they shouldn't be. While the security industry points the finger at the bad guys, or even computer users, John rightfully points the finger at the security industry. There's lots of biting criticism here that hopefully will make the industry examine itself, and lead to some positive change. It would be great to see a world where security vendors aren't feeding hackers all the ammo they need to break in to machines (which is not condoned at McAfee), and where the industry is more cooperative in general and tries to solve the problem, not just cover up its symptoms.

This book makes me feel proud, because it shows that we did our job staying ahead of the industry during my tenure as McAfee's CTO. When John complains about problems with antivirus systems, he is talking about problems that other people have, but that

McAfee has been working to solve, with industry-leading technologies such as Artemis (*http://www.mcafee.com/us/enterprise/ products/artemis_technology/index.html*). And while McAfee has changed the game with Artemis, I can say it is cooking up even better technologies that will go even beyond the vision of antivirus nirvana that John describes in this book. I am excited to see these technologies come to life, not just because they were incubated under my watch, but because they fundamentally change the playing field in the good guys' favor.

Even though I recently retired from McAfee, I still believe it is doing far better than the rest of the security industry for a few core reasons. First, it is a dedicated security company. As practice, it doesn't spread the brainpower around on other technologies, such as storage. Second, it cares about everybody who needs protection, from the consumer to the enterprise, and spends a lot of time listening closely to customers, with frequent customer councils. Third, McAfee hires the best and the brightest people in the industry. But it's not just about collecting technical talent. Yes, it has a deep bench of experts. But McAfee actually listens to them. When you spend a lot of time listening to both the experts and the people you're trying to protect, it's amazing how smart you can become, and how good of a job you can do. And creating *real* solutions to *real* problems is something that I love, not just solving symptoms.

McAfee is lucky to have such a deep bench of talent, like John Viega. John has done a phenomenal job at McAfee, helping lead the charge into many emerging areas, such as web protection, data loss prevention, and Software-as-a-Service. He has also been instrumental in pushing forward the core technologies and practices, providing McAfee with even better antivirus and even better product security than it had before he first arrived.

My philosophy is to constantly strive to be better and to always try to delight the customer. By working closely with customers, not only can one understand their pain points, but one can also create a relationship with them that not only allows, but encourages, their feedback into the development cycle. Products are not developed in a vacuum. Many other vendors just rely on their smart guys and don't talk much to customers, which creates more problems than it solves. For some companies, decision points are squarely based on dollars and company benefit. Not for me, and not for John. John always wants to do the right thing for the company *and* the customer.

For both John and myself, the customer comes first. We have always tried to do as much as we can to make the world a better place. For instance, we have pushed McAfee to distribute software at no cost, such as SiteAdvisor and our Stinger malware cleanup tool. Whereas some vendors profit while putting people at risk by making software vulnerabilities public, John and I have always pushed to do the right thing for every software user. While I was at McAfee, if an employee found a bug in someone else's code, the policy was to inform the vendor, instead of the world. (We also advised vendors not to announce the issue, though often they did.) And if something did go public, we provided free information to help people figure out if they might be at risk.

John's philosophy of doing right by the customer is spot on. I wish the entire security industry felt the same way. Maybe this book will be the kick in the pants that the rest of the industry needs.

John's leadership has left his fingerprints on all aspects of McAfee's products, in ways that provide invaluable benefit to customers. He is not afraid to do the right thing, even if it's not the popular thing. And he's not afraid to issue a "call to action" for the computer security field in general, which is what he's done with *The Myths of Security*. I just hope that the rest of the field sees this book in the same light I have, and uses it as constructive criticism to build better security for everyone. Given my extensive experience in this field over the past 15 years, there are few books that I would put into this category. When I talk with people about the computer security field, I will certainly be advising them to read this book.

—Christopher Bolin
Former CTO and Executive
Vice President of McAfee

Preface

The Myths of Security is for anyone interested in computer security, whether it's a hobby, a profession, or just something you worry about. By reading this book, you'll get some insight into what the bad guys do, as well as what the good guys (and gals) do. You'll find that good guys often do bad things—things that put everybody at risk. You'll learn about what's traditionally been wrong with the industry, and how it's slowly starting to change.

If you've picked up this book, odds are that you care about computer security a lot more than the average person. When people outside the computer industry ask me what I do, I get one of three reactions:

- They give me a disinterested look with some explanation of why they don't care. Like, "I own a Mac," or "I let my kids worry about that for me."

- They ask something like, "What should I be doing to keep myself safe?", and when I give them the answer, they change the subject, because they have gotten all the information they ever wanted to know about Internet security.

- They relate some "horror show" about their computer malfunctions and ask if I can do anything to help.

Many people are smart and computer savvy but still don't care about security, unless there's some kind of problem that might affect them. They're willing to pay a little bit so that there are no problems on their computers. But those problems shouldn't cause more problems. For example, if antivirus (AV) slows down computers too much, some people will stop using it altogether.

When you get into the IT world, a lot more people seem to be interested in security. It's like an incredibly challenging game. The bad guys are clever, and find lots of ways (often incredibly creative ways) to get around all the defenses others have erected. We need to try to build better defenses so the bad guys will be less successful.

It's not a game we'll ever win.

Imagine you're trying to protect the entire Internet, which has at least 1.6 billion users. Let's pretend that those users are all running security mechanisms that are 99.9% effective, and everybody gets attacked at least once a year. That's still over 1.6 million people infected a year.

On the good side, people aren't under constant attack. On the bad side, it doesn't take a failure in your security to get you in trouble. When there's money involved, there will always be successful criminals. And, even if there are no overt security problems with an IT system, the bad guys will just lie, cheat, and steal if that's what it takes to achieve their goals. Remember, the bad guys were successful before there were computers involved, and they will examine all their options and take the easiest path.

If all you really care to know is what you can do to protect yourself, I do cover that in Chapter 17. But, if you don't want to read that far, you'll be probably be OK if you follow these three steps:

1. Run current AV (don't ignore it when your subscription to updates runs out).

2. Always install operating system and program updates for the programs you use, as soon as you can.

3. Make sure that you are dealing with legitimate people before you do anything on the Internet, whether it be shopping online, opening a document that you received in your email, or running a program you downloaded off the Internet.

These days, you probably won't notice if you're infected unless your AV tells you, in which case it can probably clean up the infection. But if your computer seems messed up (e.g., odd crashes, running slow, too many pop-up ads), you may or may not be infected. Either way, the right thing to do is to find someone you trust who can deal with the problem for you. Maybe it's your kid, or maybe it's the Best Buy Geek Squad. In the worst-case scenario, your computer might need to be rebuilt from scratch, so it's also a good idea to keep all your data backed up (as if it wasn't a good idea anyway).

If your primary concern is keeping yourself safe, you've now learned everything you need to know, and it probably wasn't anything revolutionary. However, I hope you'll be curious enough to read a little further and learn more about the computer security industry. There's a reason why so many people in IT find it interesting, and if you keep reading, maybe you'll see it.

The security industry is large enough to rake in well over 10 billion dollars every year. There are hundreds of companies and thousands of products. Most people that use computers need to care about security. So do most companies. There's a huge portion of the IT security market that is focused on selling solutions to companies. As the companies get larger, they tend to hire someone with a bit of security knowledge who is responsible for choosing security technologies for the company. In this book, I'm not going to pay much attention to this kind of customer, one who actually has a good reason to care about IT security (keeping a job). There are plenty of myths for me to debunk in the corporate realm, but I'm typically more interested in the more mundane problems that ordinary people have.

Plus, most normal people aren't going to care about things like Sarbanes-Oxley compliance, or whether management consoles from different security vendors are able to share data.

Why Myths of Security?

It's natural that myths proliferate in a discipline as tangled and murky as computer security. In this book, I'll clear up a lot of those myths.

Most people have heard—and probably believe—some of the myths that have grown up around computer security. For instance, I've had plenty of nontechnical people ask me, "Is it true that McAfee creates the viruses they detect?" (No.) Many people have probably heard that Macs are more secure than Windows

PCs, but it's far more complicated than that. And, people assume their antivirus software is protecting them, but it's worth being skeptical about that.

People in the industry have their misconceptions, too. Everybody seems to think that the vulnerability research community is helping improve security. But it's not; it's feeding the bad guys.

I'll also discuss some of my solutions to these problems. We've come to think that many of these problems are intractable. As I've said, the bad guys have an intrinsic advantage—but that doesn't mean there aren't solutions.

Acknowledgments

As an incentive to get my mom to read this book (she is smart, but probably thinks she can ignore security because she uses a Mac), I'd like to dedicate this book to her. I've been lucky enough to have lots of great people in my life who have encouraged me and believed in me, but she's been at it the longest. And I know she does it the best, because there's nothing as strong as a parent's love for a child.

I should know, because no matter how much my daughters, Emily and Molly, insist that they love me more than I love them, I know it's just not possible. Thanks, kids, for being so awesome. You make me happier than you will ever know...unless you have your own kids someday. And, if you do, I hope you have kids that are just like you. Normally when parents say that, it's because the kids are making them suffer, and they want the kid to learn what it was like to be them. That's not true here. You kids have never made me suffer; it's always been easy being your dad. I only suffer a little, and it's because I wish we could spend even more time together than we do.

There are never enough hours in the day to get everything done. Writing a book is no exception. The time one spends writing has to come from somewhere. For me, it meant I spent less time working, and I'd like to thank Blake Watts for picking up the slack at work, for reviewing a lot of these chapters early on, and for being so positive. Oh, and for doing a great job.

Similarly, I'd like to thank my amazing girlfriend, Debbie Moynihan, for putting up with me, no matter what. I clearly haven't been the best boyfriend, working too hard at my job and on this book. But she never complained about it. Instead, she reviewed the entire manuscript. I'm a really lucky guy.

Thanks also to my good friend Leigh Caldwell, who reviewed the entire book as well. He didn't ask, but since he so generous with his time, I feel obliged to say that I love reading his economics blog: *http://www.knowingandmaking.com/*.

And, of course, I'd like to think other people who reviewed parts of this book: Christopher Hoff, George Reese, Andy Jaquith, David Coffey, Steve Mancini, and Dave at subverted.org.

Writing this book has been a blast. Every other book I've done has been really technical and required a lot of elbow grease. In this book, I've just had to share my (strong and often controversial) opinions. That's been fun, but the team I've worked with at O'Reilly has made the job even more enjoyable. My editor, Mike Loukides, has always had inspiring ideas and great feedback. When I'm behind, he's able to crack the whip in a nice way that doesn't demotivate me. Plus, he's always up for grabbing a pizza and beer. My copyeditor, Amy Thomson, was not only thorough, but she kept me laughing with all her witty comments in the margins. And, I also need to thank Mike Hendrickson (who also is good fun over a pint) for convincing me to take all my pent-up opinions and write a book, when I was going to just blog a few things.

Matt Messier, David Coffey, Leigh Caldwell, and Zach Girouard, my best friends, also deserve lots of credit for influencing my thinking (they're all at least in the software industry) and for keeping me sane while writing the book and working on a startup.

Hundreds of other people have helped influence the thinking that went into this book. It's way too many to call them all out— almost everyone I'm connected to on LinkedIn, Facebook, and Twitter is on that list. My non-techie friends deserve just as much thanks for helping shape my opinions on the world at large, and helping me relax when necessary.

When I first got into security, I was really focused on how to help developers keep security bugs out of the software they write. I branched out in a few directions on my own, but it was Christopher Bolin who believed in me enough to give me strategic responsibilities across McAfee's vast security portfolio. Because of him (and

Jeff Green, who expanded my responsibilities further still), I was in a great position to develop an even deeper understanding of both the security industry and of business in general. Most of the people I've worked with at McAfee have been incredibly sharp and incredibly giving. Thanks to everyone who continues to make McAfee an enjoyable place to work.

Though lots of people have contributed to my thinking on security, nobody is to blame for my opinions other than me. I am happy to disagree with people respectfully, and logic and facts can change my mind. If you'd like to debate anything with me respectfully, I will do my best to make time to respond. Either send me an email (*viega@list.org*), or, preferably, find me on Twitter (*@viega*).

How to Contact Us

Please address comments and questions concerning this book to the publisher:

> O'Reilly Media, Inc.
> 1005 Gravenstein Highway North
> Sebastopol, CA 95472
> 800-998-9938 (in the United States or Canada)
> 707-829-0515 (international or local)
> 707-829-0104 (fax)

We have a web page for this book, where we list examples and any plans for future editions. You can access this information at:

> *http://www.oreilly.com/catalog/9780596523022/*

You can also send messages electronically. To be put on the mailing list or request a catalog, send an email to:

> *info@oreilly.com*

To comment on the book, send an email to:

> *bookquestions@oreilly.com*

For more information about our books, conferences, Resource Centers, and the O'Reilly Network, see our website at:

> *http://www.oreilly.com*

Safari® Books Online

 When you see a Safari® Books Online icon on the cover of your favorite technology book, that means the book is available online through the O'Reilly Network Safari Bookshelf.

Safari offers a solution that's better than e-books. It's a virtual library that lets you easily search thousands of top tech books, cut and paste code examples, download chapters, and find quick answers when you need the most accurate, current information. Try it for free at *http://my.safaribooksonline.com*.

CHAPTER 1

The Security Industry Is Broken

When I was in college, I worked on the Alice project, run by Randy Pausch of "Last Lecture" fame. Alice was a system for virtual reality and 3D graphics—working on it got me the few cool points I had in college. However, the primary goal of Randy's project had nothing to do with virtual reality or being cool. It was all about making computer programming easy. Randy wanted high school kids to be able to write their own computer games without having to be computer programmers. The goal was to get them programming without noticing they were doing it.

After I got over the cool factor of fighting droids with a real light saber in a virtual reality environment (you held a flashlight in your hand, but it looked like a light saber in virtual reality), I found I wasn't actually all that passionate about computer graphics. But Randy had definitely gotten me excited about making things easy for average people.

My first introduction to Randy came when I took his Usability Engineering class, which was about making software products that are easy to use. I was struggling with whether I wanted to go into the computer field at all. I knew I was good at it, but the previous coursework I'd taken had almost scared me off because it kept me dozing off...classes like Fortran and Discrete Math.

But on the first day of class, Randy showed us a VCR and talked about how difficult it was to do simple things, like set the time. He talked about how the buttons were all clumped together in ways that made it difficult to distinguish what was what. He got everyone sharing their frustrations with their VCRs, and with plenty of other common things, such as light switches that don't turn off the light you think they should, or doors that you think you should push but actually require you to pull.

Then Randy put on goggles, pulled out a sledgehammer, and beat the crap out of the VCR. Then he proceeded to destroy other donated devices with shoddy user interfaces.

That inspired me. It made me realize that the entire consumer electronics industry and the computer software industry were fundamentally broken, because they weren't really providing people with good experiences, just passable ones. It seemed that everywhere I looked, people making products were assuming they knew their users, without spending enough time actually talking to them. Nearly 15 years later, very little has changed; the average user is still an afterthought. I've met many product managers who are supposed to figure out what to build, and only a few of them spent any significant time with their users. Most work on projects that in the grand scheme of things should be less important than embracing the customer, like helping support sales efforts or building marketing material.

Once I got out of college, I switched immediately into the security field, where I've been for about 10 years now. This field was easy to get passionate about because bad security was clearly having a negative impact on the world. Almost everyone I knew who ran Windows had some horror story about a virus deleting their files, crashing their machines, or otherwise doing something to sap productivity. In college, I'd already seen the impact of software flaws on machines connected to the Internet, having seen hackers delete content and render machines unusable, all because of some incredibly subtle problem in code written by a third party.

Very quickly, I got up to speed on the field, then started doing my best to have an impact. Along with Gary McGraw, I wrote my first book on how to keep security bugs out of software, *Building Secure Software* (Addison-Wesley; we are finally looking at doing a long-overdue revision), and a few others— I'm particularly proud of the *Secure Programming Cookbook* (O'Reilly; *http://oreilly.com/catalog/9780596003944/*). Then I started a company called Secure Software, which built tools to automatically find security problems in programs by looking at the code that developers write (that company was acquired by Fortify, and I am now on the Fortify advisory board). I then took a job as Vice President, Chief Security Architect at McAfee, which would like you to know it's the world's largest dedicated IT Security company (Symantec is several times larger, but it does a few things that aren't security, allowing McAfee to make the claim with a straight face). After a couple of years of doing a lot of merger and acquisitions work, plus managing the engineering of most of the core technologies that are shared across McAfee's products, such as the antivirus (AV) engine, I left to do another startup, and was back at McAfee within a year, this time as CTO of the Software-as-a-Service business unit.

Ten years later, the security world doesn't seem too much better for my efforts. In fact, in many ways, things have gotten worse. Sure, in part this is because lots more people are on the Internet, and computer security is an incredibly difficult thing to get right.

Still, everywhere I turn in the security world, I see, as my friend Mark Curphey likes to say, "security bullshit." This industry is not focused on providing users a good experience with its products. But even worse, it is not really focused on providing the more secure experience that is implicitly promised.

For instance, look at the bedrock of the computer security industry, the piece that more or less everybody feels they need to have: AV. Most normal people think that AV solutions don't work very well. And, for the most part, that's right (even though AV vendors are continually trying to improve their products). These solutions are often 15 years old, and address the problems of that time, not this one. Most of the major players could have been doing a much better job for a long time, but inertia has kept everyone running crapware that takes up too much of your system's resources to stop probably less than half of all potential infections.

Like Randy Pausch smashing a VCR, I'd like to help people realize what is wrong with the industry, and I am hoping to inspire at least a couple of people to put customers first in their business pursuits in the security world.

In this book, I'm going to spend a lot of time sharing my perspective on the industry. As much as I can, I'll try not only to identify the glaring problems that I see, but also to show what the industry can do differently.

For the most part, my criticisms will apply to most companies, but not all. For instance, I have been very happy with McAfee's technological progress over the past few years. In general, it has listened to me and to a lot of other smart people, including its customers. I'll try not to promote McAfee too much, but in many cases, you can bet that the problems I discuss have been considered there, and we've either addressed them or we plan to address them.

I don't believe that there is a "silver bullet" for security, but I do think that end users should be getting a lot more for their money, including a better experience (like AV that doesn't slow down their computers) and better security (like AV that is more than one step above "worthless"). A lot of little things are just fundamentally wrong, and the industry as a whole is broken.

CHAPTER 2

Security: Nobody Cares!

Why don't the masses think too highly of the IT (information technology) security market? It wasn't too long ago that every major news source reported about computer security problems on a regular basis. In 2001, the entire world heard about Code Red, Nimda, and Code Red II. But the level of coverage surrounding computer security issues has dropped steadily in the 7+ years since. Since Zotob in early 2005 (which was a minor story in comparison to the stories of 2001), nothing's really come close to the level of coverage, even though the Storm Worm has been far more widespread a problem.

Actually, that was true when I started writing this book, but as I finish it, the Conficker worm has been saturating technology publications for the last six months. Everybody in the security field has heard about it, and many information technologists have as well. I've been polling friends and family about it, and I have found that people who do a good job of keeping up with news don't know about it, which means if they did see an article about Conficker, they probably skipped it. Even my technical friends seem blasé about it, and many of the ones who would care have long since switched to the Mac.

Today, the tech world might hear a lot about security issues, but the world at large rarely does. That's not because of a lack of security problems. Certainly, the amount of malware has been on an exponential growth curve for a few years, as there is a lot of money to be made in malware. With this big malware economy, why isn't this a common mainstream topic? Well, the press doesn't report on it because people don't care anymore, and the less the press reports, the less people care, creating a nice downward spiral into ignorance. That said, there are plenty of other factors keeping people from caring about the topic:

Malware likes to stay hidden
> For a while, if you were infected, you would probably end up with an incredibly slow computer and tons of ads popping up all over the place. It didn't take long for malware writers to figure out that they weren't going to make as much money off a user if the infection was obvious and the user paid to get the thing cleaned. So these days, Malware typically tries to do its thing without being obvious. Even when malware delivers ads, it usually isn't going to overwhelm you with them. You might get occasional pop ups, but not a sea of them. Or you might have legitimate ads silently replaced with the ones that the malware would like to deliver. As a result, people don't notice many infections, so the consumer perception is that either their security software is doing its job or there just isn't much of a problem.

Security products aren't top of mind
> Let's assume that desktop security solutions actually work well (even though this isn't a very good assumption). With traditional AV, it could be that the product is working well, proactively stopping bad stuff from executing on your computer. The typical consumer will never see the AV software working, and won't give it any credit.

The consequences haven't been too bad
> A lot of consumers expected an Internet apocalypse, where some large chunk of the people they knew would have their bank accounts drained and their identities stolen. For a while, people were afraid of doing commerce on the Net. The people who were most afraid just refused to buy things online. Everyone else has been somewhat consoled because credit card companies will carry the bulk of liability. Plus, not only have things like card theft not taken off, but when someone's identity is stolen, it isn't always clear that it was done on a computer.

For instance, if you're in the U.S. and someone steals your credit card number, it is more likely that the theft occurred in a restaurant, where someone wrote down your card information when he or she took it to the back to swipe it.

The story is boring

To the average person, Code Red, Nimda, and the like were all approximately the same story. Computer security issues don't make good headlines because too much sounds the same as the last incident. Yes, there might be minor variations in who is affected, what the malware is doing, and how fast it is spreading, but particularly when you (as an average person) assume you're not at specific risk, eventually you're just going to stop reading these stories, and so reporters are going to stop writing them—reporting is a business and the money comes from following the stories people want to read.

The security industry isn't too credible

People aren't going to pay attention in a world where everyone seems to "know" that, for example, AV solutions "mostly don't work" and that they "slow your computer to a crawl." Whether or not there is truth to such things (there is), the security industry doesn't have much credibility (I can't tell you how many times people have asked me in all honesty whether McAfee writes viruses so it can have something to detect). So if a story is vendor-focused, it's not going to be too believable.

Let's face it: computer security is a great big yawner to the world at large. Whether or not there is a big problem (there is), it just doesn't seem to matter to people. This means the general public is largely uninformed, and this has some consequences for the industry:

- Consumers can't tell the difference between security products. They typically expect one product that does everything.

- Consumers aren't willing to pay much for security products. Even though they do expect to buy one product that does everything, they feel like they're getting ripped off by being forced into buying full suites, where they don't know what the real difference is between the entry-level functionality and the premium functionality. The perceived value is low and people expect that they're getting a lot of functionality they don't use.

- It does seem like people generally feel that AV is a "must have" (particularly on Windows), but do not have much confidence in its ability to protect them.

One interesting consequence is that many people out there don't pay attention to whether they actually have working AV or not. Lots of people get their AV from a major manufacturer as an OEM (original equipment manufacturer) preinstall (meaning it came with the PC they bought from Dell, HP, Gateway, or whomever). They assume that they get it for free, for life. However, most of these preinstalls are for a limited time, usually no more than a year. When users get to the end of the free period, they often do not renew. There are many reasons for this, but commonly people ignore the nagging pop-up balloons in the Taskbar, and then either don't notice when protection expires or forget about it.

There aren't really any easy solutions for improving public perception. I think consumer protection is rapidly plummeting in perceived value, particularly with reasonable traction from free AV solutions, like AVG, Avira, and Avast (sorry, open source world, ClamAV doesn't register). Even though the free AV vendors have poor brands, they have enough users that it shows that people are starting to shift away from brand-based decisions and toward price-based decisions. That's not to say that I think better brands necessarily produce better products, it's just that going with a big brand is a shortcut to doing the research. Consumers assume a big brand will be competent enough, or else it wouldn't be successful.

No, I think the road is going to be long and hard. There are a lot of problems, many of which I'm going to explore in later chapters.

CHAPTER 3

It's Easier to Get "Owned" Than You Think

I know a lot of arrogant geeks. They think they're never going to get hit by malware because they are so technically savvy, and they will never let themselves be in harm's way. They are wrong.

Similarly, I know a lot of arrogant computer users, geeks or not. They include the legions of Apple users who think that the company's OS X operating system is magically better than the major alternative. They include the people who have bought into similar marketing from Microsoft about Vista being the most secure operating system ever.

Such people believe what the bad guys would have them believe!

Let's look at common ways to get "0wned," and we'll see that in some cases, it's a lot easier than most people would expect.

First, getting "0wned" can generally mean one of several things. It might mean you end up with bad software (malware—short for "malicious software") installed on your computer. Or, it might mean that your online banking details go out the door to a stranger, whether or not you end up with malware on your machine.

Let's start with infections (installs of malicious software). One particularly common way to get infected with malware is to install it yourself. You might click on a link in an email message, thinking it's a legitimate URL when it isn't. Or you might download an application off the Internet that you think is legitimate, when in fact it is malware.

There are lots of deception techniques to try to make people download bad stuff. You can try to make people think they're downloading something they actually want to download. For instance, imagine 18-year-old males searching the Web for the celebrity sex tape of the day. They find one site through Google that claims to have it for free, but it requires a plug-in for Windows Media Player that they don't have. When they "click here" to get the plug-in (Figure 3-1), they end up installing malware. This is even more effective if the download installs both the malware and a legitimate plug-in, then plays the video!

Figure 3-1. Malware can masquerade as a legitimate download, such as Windows Media Player

There are lots of popular download categories that tend to bundle malware, such as screensavers. The big screensaver sites all have some screensavers that bundle adware or spyware. And, if you search for the coolest new pop culture icon of the day, anything executable you might download (like a game) is immediately suspect.

OK, if you're an übergeek, you might think that you are better than that. You don't download stuff unless it comes from a reputable vendor and you can see plainly that lots of other people have downloaded it. Score a point for yourself. Nevertheless, there are plenty of situations where you could think you're downloading one application but you're really downloading another, like when there's a bad guy on your local network launching a *man-in-the-middle* attack or performing a DNS cache poisoning attack on you (don't worry if you don't know what these things are; it isn't important for this discussion). Fortunately, those are rare occurrences.

Another way people get "0wned" regularly is by having a bad guy take advantage of security problems on their systems, especially in software that is Internet-capable, such as web browsers. Web browsers are massive pieces of code and they're bound to have security problems, no matter how hard people look (a topic I'll cover in great detail later in this book).

But there are websites out there that might try to break in to your computer by using a security problem in the browser. If you browse the wrong website with a vulnerable browser and operating system configuration, you'll likely end up with malware installed (a "drive-by download").

Browsers aren't the only programs that can be vulnerable. There have been problems in desktop applications, such as Microsoft Word, in which opening a malicious data file will also install malware. There have also been prominent security holes in Microsoft *services* (programs that run even when the user isn't in front of the computer; usually, they allow programs on other machines to connect and talk to the machine on which they run) and other important third-party software where the service is sitting on your machine waiting for other people to connect to it. The bad guys just have to be in a position to talk to that service, then they can break in to your machine with no intervention required from you.

A couple of technologies (such as firewalls) keep random Joes on the Internet from being able to see vulnerable services, but there are plenty of other cases where there's risk. For example, if your computer is sitting on a corporate network, often all the machines on the corporate network can talk to one another with no problem. If a bad guy has control of any of the machines on that network that can see you, and you have a vulnerable service running on your machine, you are at risk. However, these days, few services are visible by default, other than general networking services (and on Windows, these have certainly had big problems in the past).

Even if you're not running a vulnerable browser or in a position where some other software can be exposed, it's easy to be tricked by things that look legitimate but aren't. For instance, if you happen to type in a bad domain name or otherwise navigate to the wrong link, you might get a fake error claiming that malware is keeping you from loading a link, and a dialog box that looks like it is coming from Windows will try to install AV or antispyware software that really isn't (Figures 3-2 and 3-3).

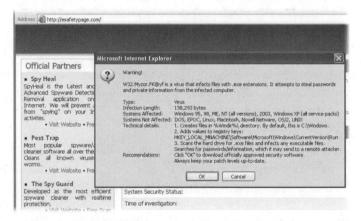

Figure 3-2. *Some malware distributors trick users into downloading fake AV software with legitimate-looking dialog boxes like this one*

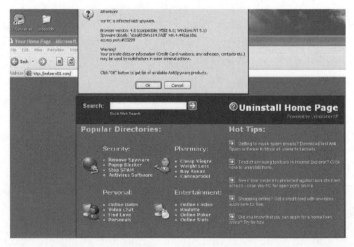

Figure 3-3. *This dialog box claims to provide links to antispyware, while it actually contains a link to malware*

Or you might get another fake pop up that looks like it's coming from Windows, enticing you to install something, which you may install because you think Microsoft is suggesting it (Figure 3-4).

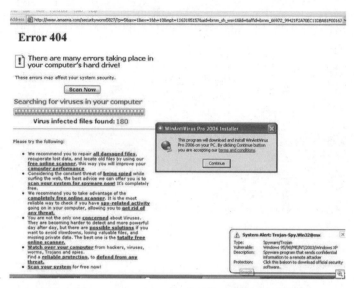

Figure 3-4. This fake pop-up error looks like a Windows message

Sometimes these fake messages from Microsoft offer you a range of options in an attempt to look more reputable (Figure 3-5).

Most of the arrogant geeks I know still wouldn't be bothered by the status quo. They would claim that they don't browse to any risky sites, they either don't need security software or only run software from reputable vendors, and they run "personal firewalls" that are designed to make sure their machines don't accept unsolicited traffic, even if the software services they're running are infected.

They also don't expect that they would fall for *phishing* scams. These kinds of people have trained themselves to ignore email messages from eBay unless their user ID is explicitly called out in it (when bad guys are spamming lots of people with fake eBay messages, they usually don't call out individual eBay usernames, because they don't know them). Similarly, they don't download "postcards from a friend!" unless the friend's name is clearly spelled out. But I still know a few previously arrogant geeks who have been taken in by phishing scams.

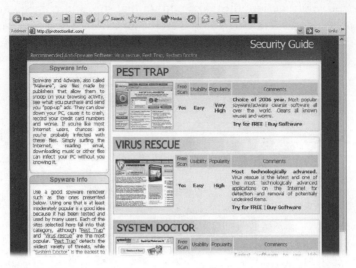

Figure 3-5. *Another fake message to dupe users into downloading malware*

Phishers tend to use techniques that work, but they occasionally shift gears. For example, a few weeks before I wrote this, phishers started sending messages claiming that the receiver had a UPS package that couldn't be delivered. The message looked like it came from UPS and asked the receiver to provide correct personal details so the package could be delivered. Since it was a new technique, a few pretty savvy people fell victim.

But the bad guys have a few more tricks up their sleeves. One technique is called *spearphishing*, which is basically customizing phishing attempts to individual companies or even individual people. You might get an email message that seems to come from your corporate IT people, asking you to log in to a web portal to change your password because it's about to expire. Of course, if the mail comes from a bad guy, the site will be fake and the purpose will be to capture your current password, not to change it.

Spearphishing can easily be used to target individuals and networks of friends. For instance, let's say that you'd like to send me a targeted phishing attempt. First, you can easily get a few of my email addresses just by having my name. Similarly, if you happen to be a bad guy who has my email address because you bought it off some list, you can easily find my name with a little bit of web searching (which can be automated).

Let's say you'd like to trick me into downloading some malware, and you think it might be good to disguise it as a postcard from one of my friends. We can easily use Facebook for this. First, let's search for my name (Figure 3-6).

Figure 3-6. *Step 1 of our experimental scam: use Facebook to gather information about a potential victim*

That's great; there's only one result. Let's view my friends (Figure 3-7). To do this, I created a temporary account with no friends that I deleted after this experiment.

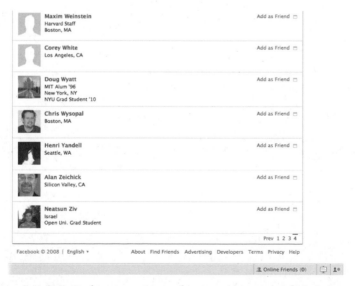

Figure 3-7. *Step 2 of our experimental scam: view potential victim's friends on Facebook*

Great, now you've got a couple hundred names you could claim the postcard might be from. If you claim to live in Boston, MA, you can now suddenly see my entire profile and pick up all sorts of personal tidbits to figure out how to target me, from my status messages to my work history. Figure 3-8 shows an example of my profile, as seen by an anonymous user with no friends, claiming to live in Boston.

Figure 3-8. Step 3 of our experimental scam: access potential victim's Facebook profile to gather information

These are all default Facebook settings. You can hide your friend list from strangers, but you have to go out of your way to do it, and few people do.

Bad guys can easily scrape this kind of information automatically. While legitimate sites like Facebook try to detect people who are pulling off too much information, bad guys can grab little bits of information at a time without getting caught, and can then send far fewer targeted email messages that will have a much higher chance of success than a blanket mass-email campaign.

Maybe some of my more arrogant geek acquaintances would tell me they wouldn't open up a postcard even if it came from their mothers or girlfriends (who you're dating usually shows up to people in the same city). They may feel immune to everything they've read so far. No amount of social engineering is going to fool them!

And as we've said, they would never browse to risky sites. But would they browse to MLB.com (the home of Major League Baseball) or the Economist, or geek sites like Slashdot?

All of those sites are established and well respected, yet they could be the places where you end up getting infected. Bad guys buy legitimate ads on major sites, then occasionally sneak in some evil stuff, like an ad for a fake AV product that turns out to be spyware. Or, it may be an ad that looks legitimate but tries to exploit your browser. And this could happen on any site that serves ads from a major network, like CNN.com. Sure, advertising networks try to keep this kind of stuff out, but it can often be difficult, particularly when you realize that ads are often composed of code, not just static pictures. Many ads are developed in ActionScript, a programming language by Adobe.

If you don't think you're vulnerable to an ad on your favorite website running a browser exploit, then you're a very arrogant geek. I suspect you fall into one of these two categories:

- You think you could never get tricked, and you go out of your way to make sure you're always running the most recent versions of your browser.

- You think you're safe because you're using Apple or a Linux system, or maybe an odd-duck browser like Opera, or you think you're doing something else unusual enough to keep you safe.

If you fall into the first category and you really are diligent about it, your only real worry is when a bad guy starts using a "zero day" exploit against your browser, meaning (more or less) that the browser vendor hadn't fixed the problem before the exploit started going wild. Thankfully, that doesn't happen too much.

If you fall into the second category, just realize that you're relying on being an economically unattractive target to bad guys, meaning it's far cheaper for them to find victims elsewhere. That might not always be true. Apple users in particular should be worried, as I'll soon discuss.

CHAPTER 4

It's Good to Be Bad

In this chapter we'll look at what motivates bad guys to break in to computers, and what's going on inside their heads. It used to be that people created viruses and worms for silly reasons: perhaps just to prove to themselves or their friends that they are clever, or perhaps because they want to cause misery. There aren't too many people like that in the world.

No, most people on the dark side of the force are there for one reason: easy money!

Let's say you're a bad guy and you get some bad software onto somebody's machine. What kinds of things could you do to make money? Here's a short list that is by no means exhaustive:

- You could collect credit card numbers and the data associated with it (such as the CVV validation code). You could collect the data as users enter it into e-commerce shopping sites, then sell it off to other bad guys. Eventually someone might use the credit card information for a day or maybe just for the occasional single transaction, in hopes the credit card holder will never notice the fraud.

- You could wait until people use their online banking sites, then sniff important account information (such as username, password, account number, and so on), or even take over the connection when the machine goes idle so that you can move money around.

- You could collect any kind of account information. If you collect valid credentials to large corporate networks, for instance, you might suspect that there's a black market for that kind of thing. Even for regular old PCs, you could sell the account information to people who want to run some of these other scams.

- You could wait for people to buy stuff from an online merchant, like Amazon.com, and trick the online merchant into thinking that you referred the user to Amazon to buy a particular item, when in reality, the user went there by himself. This attack doesn't harm the user at all, just the merchant, since it ends up paying out a commission to someone who doesn't deserve it.

- You could send spam from an infected computer. You might wonder why somebody would do this. If bad guys only spam from a few places, it's easy to find and stop the sources, but if spam is sent through millions of PCs, many of them doing mostly legitimate stuff, it's a much tougher nut to crack.

- You could deliver ads to users that they wouldn't otherwise have gotten. This is the model of many adware companies. They often sell cheap ads to legitimate businesses. The legitimate businesses don't know how the companies get users to click on ads, they just care that the clicks occur.

- You could fraudulently generate "clicks" for ads in order to generate revenue for your own site, which does nothing but serve up a ton of ads. You put up your big web page of ads, you have infected computers click the ads on those pages (the infected user doesn't even have to see the pages), and the ad network will pay you the referral fee for the click. Or, if your business has a competitor, you could click on all your competitors' links to eat up their advertising budget, taking away their "real" traffic (most ad campaigns stop when the budget is used up).

- Similarly, you could replace all the ads that were supposed to be delivered to a user with ads that are served up from your home page. This closely mimics "real" traffic, making it even tougher for ad networks like Google to detect the fraud.

- If the user's PC is connected to an active modem, you could dial a premium 1-900 number (like a psychic hotline), and cause the modem to dial it. You could then take advantage of the phone call time, but the call would be billed to the user. Or, if you own the 1-900 number, you would get all the money. Generally, you would want to keep calls short and few, so that people won't notice or won't complain if they do notice.

- If you've got a large number of infected computers under your control, you could take money from other people to try to "take down" popular websites using a so-called distributed denial-of-service (DDOS) attack. There's probably not a big market for this, but this kind of denial-of-service (DOS) attack does happen occasionally. It's probably most often caused by bad guys with political agendas, or just people looking to make mischief.

- You could use an infected computer to attack another computer. You could break in to other computers on your network and use any of the aforementioned techniques to make money on those new computers you've infected.

- You could hold important data for ransom (such as personal photos, locally stored email messages, music files, and video). This is usually done by encrypting files on the computer so that the victim can't access them until he gets the decryption key.

The more computers a bad guy has, the better off he is in terms of making money. Having more computers makes it easier to get spam through, and to keep generating fraudulent clicks if the work across is distributed as many machines as possible so that no single machine is doing too much work.

A lot of bad guys end up installing general-purpose software that they can control remotely to do whatever they want. The industry calls such software *botnet software* (*bot* is a short form of "robot," indicating that the infected computer will probably run automated software to do the bad guy's nefarious bidding).

Clearly, it's in the bad guy's economic best interests if the victim doesn't know his or her computer has been taken over. There's a lot the bad guy can do to use a victim's computer to make money, without the victim having to know that the bad guy's on there. The less intrusive a bad guy is, the better off he is. So, in this day and age, when a computer is infected, it's probably the case that the bad guy only wants to slowly and unnoticeably drain money from the machine's owner, because he doesn't want to get kicked off the machine! If the bad guy does something extreme like hold files hostage (so-called *ransomware*), he may never get the money, and if he does give the files back, the machine will probably be cleaned up afterward, making it difficult to further monetize the machine. Therefore, ransomware isn't too popular.

I'd expect this to be the kind of thing bad guys would try to do as a last resort—if their primary malware is detected and removed, some secondary ransomware can hold the machine's data hostage as a last resort.

All in all, being a bad guy on the Internet pays! It's a lot easier than traditional crime, for a couple of major reasons:

- The bad guys don't have to be physically near their victims to commit crimes against them. In fact, a lot of computer crime is launched from countries like Russia and China, where both computer crime laws and enforcement of those laws are weak. If crime crosses jurisdictional boundaries, it becomes a lot harder to find and punish the bad guys.

- It's a lot easier to leave no real evidence behind. While computers do have addresses that can be used to track them to a certain degree, there are a lot of things a bad guy can do to cover his tracks. For instance, some systems allow people to do things over the Internet anonymously.

At the end of the day, computer crime is a lot cheaper for the bad guy than other kinds of crime, if the bad guy has the technical skills to pull it off. And there are plenty of ways to make lots of money without stealing it directly from end users (such as click fraud, where you end up stealing from corporations in small amounts). Plus, not too many people get caught. No wonder it is a reasonably popular and attractive profession in countries whose economies don't offer many high-paying career opportunities.

CHAPTER 5

Test of a Good Security Product: Would I Use It?

There are way too many security products and companies, and there are far too few good ones. If I see a good product, I will actually run it.

Here are some of the IT security solutions I have used in the past five years:

- SSH, the ubiquitous remote login utility, which allows me to run commands on remote machines via a text interface.

- SMTPS and S-IMAP, protocol extensions for SMTP (Simple Mail Transfer Protocol) and IMAP (Internet Message Access Protocol), to allow my mail client to talk to my email server with authentication and data security.

- Plenty of RSA tokens and HID badges (RSA and HID are companies that have lots of products for proving your identity to help you access whatever resource, be it a computer system or a door).

- Some antispam stuff (including SpamAssassin); none of it has solved my spam problem. For some of my accounts, I get so much spam that I still have to sort through hundreds of messages a day. For all other addresses, I get basically no spam, and the antispam tools just mark a few things that I probably wanted to see, and hide them for me in a junk folder.

- SiteAdvisor, for when I want to download some software from a site whose reputation I'm unsure of. I would have the plug-in installed, but there's no public plug-in available for my browser/platform combo (though SiteAdvisor for Safari on OS X will come out shortly after this book goes to print). So I go to siteadvisor.com and look up site reports manually. Don't try to switch me to Firefox; I try it every year or so, and still don't like it.

- I've been forced to run god-awful VPN (virtual private network) software at work (usually the crappy Cisco client). This allows me to access my company's resources even when I'm not actually in the office.

Here are some prominent things that I don't run:

- **Firewalls.** Firewalls can block Internet traffic, usually based on where it's going to or coming from. I'd consider firewalls important in many enterprise contexts, because people typically leave lots of vulnerable services on machines that are directly accessible to a lot of people. But in my home environment, my cable modem and wireless router both are capable of network address translation (NAT), meaning my computers are not directly accessible. The only things people on the outside can see are the things they would see anyway, because my machines are initiating the connections. On my personal server, I just don't expose ports I don't want hit. When I used to run my own firewall, I tried a number of things, but primarily used OpenBSD's PF (packet filter).

- **Antivirus (AV).** Even though I used to run development for McAfee's core AV technology, I did not use the product. I do not use the technology on a day-to-day basis. Part of this was because I use a Mac. Still, even when I run Windows, I'm just careful in what I do, and don't run AV. These aren't the right decisions for everybody. I'll explore the AV and the Mac issue later.

- **Personal firewalls.** These are like regular firewalls, but they live on your machine and give you control over which network connections to allow or to deny. Like most people, I find personal firewalls to be way too spammy to be useful.

- **Virtualization.** There are a bunch of products that try to make it look like each application runs on its own machine, so if a bad guy takes over one application, it doesn't affect everything else (e.g., GreenBorder and Returnil). Maybe someday these tools will be good, but right now, this stuff causes me too much effort (moving crap between virtual containers) to be worth the benefit.

- Any other consumer security product.

I'm largely ignoring the question of what I'd run if I owned enterprise IT. I only detailed enterprise things that got pushed down on me as an end user.

If I made technology decisions for a big company, I'd probably want to try to enforce AV and require my users to encrypt all the data on their laptops to minimize risks to the company when a laptop gets lost or stolen. There are lots of decisions that would make sense for a corporation but not for a consumer.

Let's look in a bit more detail at the "whys" for all of these technology decisions. A lot of the technology I use is authentication technology, which solves a critical need (people knowing who they're dealing with or what machines they're logged into). And, except for some setup and some password typing, all of these things work seamlessly. Heck, particularly with applications that remember my passwords for me, it's seamless enough that I forget that I, of course, use password security on pretty much any app that hits the network, like instant messaging, Twitter, Facebook, and so on. And, when there's authentication, encryption should be free and totally transparent, whether offered via SSL (Secure Sockets Layer, which is how Internet connections commonly get encrypted) or through some other cryptographic protocol.

I don't like stuff that gets in the way of my doing what I want to do. That sounds like I'm going against my own best interests, but a personal firewall that gives me pop ups every five minutes actually makes me *less* secure: after the first 20 times it is wrong, I stop reading, and start clicking "yes" to everything. But I still would feel like I was secure. Instead, I live with a reasonable sense of paranoia.

I want to use host-based security technologies (meaning stuff that runs on your computer instead of somewhere on your network—stuff like AV), because I do realize that even with me being highly vigilant, there are plenty of ways I can get hosed, including exploits and malware bundled with legitimate software. But I haven't been able to bring myself to run commercial AV products. The conventional wisdom there is right—they don't catch very much and they tend to slow down machines. Some AV products do work better than others for both accuracy and performance, but I have yet to find a good solution for my Mac.

The average nontechnical user should probably be running AV because it is pretty unobtrusive, it does catch some things, and nontechnical users don't have a good sense of what the real risks are. However, many technical people are like me—we're only going to adopt security technology if it's easy to use and works pretty well, unless forced to do so by our bosses.

CHAPTER 6

Why Microsoft's Free AV Won't Matter

Microsoft recently announced that it's going to stop selling its consumer security product OneCare; instead, it's going to give the product away.

I've had several people ask me questions including, "Why would Microsoft do that?" and, "Do you think McAfee and Symantec are scared?" I recently read an article (*http://news.cnet.com/8301-10789_3-10102154-57.html*) that said:

> With traditional antivirus protection perhaps becoming obsolete, maybe it's time that Symantec and McAfee start offering free versions of their own antivirus products—something that I've said for years.

That's absurd.

AV vendors certainly were worried stiff when Microsoft first entered the AV market. They assumed that Microsoft would do the same thing it does in every other market—dominate it and drive everyone else out.

The big vendors started focusing on how they could make up for the revenue loss that they considered inevitable. They felt that while Microsoft could trounce their consumer business, they would not be in a good position to meet enterprise needs any time soon (and there is some truth to that).

Starting with the Veritas acquisition, Symantec began acquiring its way into adjacent markets to diversify its revenue and beef up its enterprise business. While McAfee already had a strong enterprise offering, it focused on protecting its consumer market share by striking big OEM preinstall deals with major PC manufacturers like Dell. McAfee paid a lot of money up front for this positioning in the hopes of retaining market share and recouping the money on the back end.

Yes, the AV industry was running scared for a long time. But what happened? Quite simply, Microsoft's entry into the AV market fizzled.

It's not for lack of trying on Microsoft's part. When it started out not doing well in competitive testing, it spent an awful lot of money beefing up its signature writing capabilities by hiring the best and the brightest. It hired key people from major competitors. It spent tons of money on marketing.

And at the end of the day, the threat never materialized. While I haven't seen recent market share data, as of January 2007, Microsoft was struggling to claim just 1% of the market (.08% according to analyst firm Piper Jaffray). I see no evidence that Microsoft has made any strides since then—the business has been a resounding failure.

Microsoft spent the money, and in relatively short order had a product that was just as good as any of its competitors' (not significantly better or revolutionary, just competitive). It built a large team. It spent a lot on marketing. But the people never came.

What went wrong?

First, the world has long held the perception that Microsoft is bad at security. Microsoft has been trying hard for most of this decade to change that perception, investing billions in product security. I'm sure it hoped that if it could field a competitive AV product, it would improve that perception. It certainly didn't make the heavy investment in AV for the money; it was a small market opportunity by Microsoft standards, not enough to be worth the large investment just for a business that would have taken at least a decade to grow to be even 1% of its (current) revenue. Yes, the $6 billion AV market is tiny when you compare it to, say, the video game market.

I expect the primary reason why Microsoft would want to keep a scaled-down business and give away a free version is for community goodwill, to slowly and steadily continue to build the perception that it is at least competent at security, and not actively bad at it.

But, let's assume for a moment that end users stop thinking Microsoft actively sucks at security. They still won't positively associate Microsoft with security. Most people won't ever know that Microsoft's AV is on par with most of the big players, and even better than some.

That will always be true, because Microsoft isn't a security vendor. People (particularly consumers) tend to think that dedicated security vendors are going to do a better job than a company whose primary function isn't security. Vendors who do lots of different things are rarely the best at anything, and people generally know this.

Even when Microsoft came in at low prices, people still thought that security was important enough that they should go with a more trusted name. People who were really concerned by price started moving to other cheap options, but ones offered by dedicated security companies, like AVG.

It's not that people don't trust Microsoft specifically to do a good job at security, it's that they don't trust anybody to do security well unless it is their primary business. Even if Microsoft goes out and buys a bunch of small security companies with good technology, perceptions won't change, and few people will use Microsoft's technology.

Microsoft never had a chance. I think the core objection will hold true when its free product comes out. I certainly wouldn't be quaking in my boots if I were McAfee or Symantec. People who want free AV already have free options, such as Avira and AVG.

The suggestion that big guys like McAfee and Symantec will have to give up on consumer revenue and give away their consumer AVs for free is absurd. If I were those companies, would I want to jump off a cliff by volunteering to cut 40+% of revenue by giving away something that plenty of people will always be happy to pay for? Absolutely not.

Yes, some price-sensitive people who can get over putting their faith in an untrusted brand (or at least, one that's unknown to them) will take their business to free vendors. And free AV might start to see enough growth that consumer revenue will shrink for the big companies. I don't see that day being close, however. The growth rate of new PCs is far outpacing the growth of free AV converts, which means the paid consumer market is still growing.

If I were a big vendor, I'd even be worried about giving away a free, "lite" version of my product. I think people would assume that since a well-known security vendor produces the product, it must provide them with the core protection they need and that everything in the paid version is just bells and whistles. Until the free AV market poses some kind of significant threat, vendors shouldn't risk giving away money. Instead, they should continue to do exactly what they've been doing since Microsoft's original wake-up call—invest in moving into adjacent growth areas.

Google Is Evil

To most engineers, Google is this wonderful playground where you get to go work on cool projects that people might actually use, and work on whatever project tickles your fancy one day a week (they call this "20% time"). Meanwhile, Google gives you free food and drink, has massages available in the office, provides lots of games, and generally encourages creativity and fun.

If you search for the phrase, "I love Google," (in quotes) you will get about 123,000 results (searching through Google, of course). I think that's pretty impressive—searching for "I love Microsoft" turns up only about 63,000 results, "I love Zac Efron" (star of the *High School Musical* franchise) turns up a mere 33,500, and "I love John Viega" returns no hits whatsoever.

Google may not love me, but I do love Google, and use its offerings extensively. Still, I often find myself agreeing with the approximately 43,200 web pages that state, "Google is evil," despite Google's corporate motto, "Don't be evil."

I don't think any particular individuals working for the company are evil (although there are probably a few). But if you look at what Google does, the net result isn't always good for the end user. It may be good for Google's shareholders, and thus the right thing for the company to do, but it's not the right thing for the rest of the world. While there are lots of things that make Google evil, I'm going to focus on why Google is actively making the world a less safe place.

And before I begin, yes, I know that Google cares a lot about security. I have some friends who have been working on security stuff there for a long time. I know Google bought Postini (a company that does spam filtering), and has done good things with it (though it has done nothing with its acquisition of consumer security company Green Border—it didn't even put it into the Google Pack, a collection of free software that doesn't do a particularly good job with security). I know Google has pretty good internal development practices, at least compared to most companies. Again, I do like Google (I use it extensively for searching), and it does many good things, but it also has evil inside it—one particular evil that is making the world a less reasonable place.

The previous chapter talked a little bit about click fraud, where a bad guy generates false clicks on ads that he hosts in order to get the commission from people clicking on the ads. Since Google provides the largest ad network in the world, it is the biggest target out there for this type of fraud. While Google does take some measures against this kind of thing (which I'll discuss shortly), my theory is that Google clearly avoids approaches that would be far better for the public, because they are not in the company's financial interests.

Let's look a bit more closely at click fraud. We'll start with Google's model. Companies with products to advertise will pay Google to place their ads. They pay Google each time their ads actually get clicked. Google can show ads in search results, or it can also show the ads through other websites. Other websites agree to show Google ads, because Google will pay for each click on an ad that comes from a site. Advertisers buy ads through the Google AdWords program. People with websites rent out space for ads through the AdSense program.

The possibilities for fraud here are many. For example, you may have seen websites displaying Google ads, where the website owner says something like, "help support this site by clicking on our ads!" That's a form of fraud, because the owner is asking people to click without any intention of buying. And it happens to be against the Google terms of service, so don't do it!

But the typical fraud goes something like this: a bad guy sets up a website with a bit of real content on a topic for which related AdSense keywords will pay out pretty well, at least a dollar per click. Then, she[1] finds a community of people doing the same thing, and they all visit one another's sites, occasionally clicking on ads.

The bad guy can't just visit her own site, because Google will determine pretty quickly that all the clicks are coming from one place and are clearly fraudulent.

If the group of con artists (sometimes called a *click farm*) isn't big enough, it probably isn't too hard for Google to catch on. But many international organized crime rings try to recruit large numbers of people in third-world countries to do the clicking, having them spend about two hours a day clicking at reasonable rates to give the illusion that sites are real sites serving real content.

Google will try to analyze trends that seem abnormal. For instance, if the bad guy clicks on too many ads compared to the number she is served, she can expect Google to catch on. And if she starts clicking on location-specific ads from all over the world, Google will probably get suspicious. One goal of the bad guys, then, is to make the traffic look as legitimate as possible without having to figure out how to get the actual traffic. Incidentally, this is also why the bad guy has to have some legitimate content—she has to expect that Google is monitoring the pages to see if she's trying one of these scams.

But if the bad guy happens to run a small botnet, she can certainly use it to generate some false clicks. She doesn't even need a very popular site. For instance, she can advertise on a keyword that has an extraordinarily high price. One popular piece of malware made false clicks on a website the bad guys had set up, with ads targeting the keyword "mesothelioma," which is a rare form of cancer caused by prolonged exposure to asbestos. Lawyers are happy to pay a lot of money for clicks, because lawsuits in this area can pay out big bucks. So, one fraudulent click could easily

---

[1] OK, this "bad guy" is apparently a bad girl. My editor is changing some of my references from "he" to "she" to make things more gender neutral. Yes, it's true that women can be criminals, but let's be honest...most of the time, only guys are stupid enough!

be worth from $5 to well north of $10. Let's say that the bad guy wants to stay under the radar but still make a decent amount of money. And let's say she's got about 10,000 computers on her botnet at any given time (this is about average for a botnet). She could have a few thousand of those computers visit her own "cancer blog" on a regular basis (varying it daily or monthly, to give the illusion of real traffic). She'd probably make sure to only have sites hit the blog where the endpoint machine is in a country where people speak English well. With each page hit, Google will serve up ads. Then, a mere 20 times a day (on average), she actually has one of the bots in the network click on an ad at random and navigate around the site a little bit to make it look like a real person is doing the navigating.

At just 20 ad clicks a day getting 10 dollars per ad, she could make $73,000 a year. That's a princely sum for somebody living in Russia, where the average income is still less than $10,000 annually, and it requires very little work.

A really clever bad guy will keep a legitimate cancer blog and invest some time in marketing it so that she gets a small readership. Then, if her botnet is ever discovered, she can claim that someone was trying to get her knocked off AdSense due to some personal grudge, maybe for some controversial views in the blog.

Google does try hard to find fraudsters. It analyzes the requests for ads and the clicks that arise. It looks for anomalies using all the data it can collect, including the Internet address for the computer requesting ads. It is quick to shut down AdSense accounts for which it can conclusively demonstrate fraud. And when Google finds fraudulent clicks, it refunds money to the people who bought the advertising.

When you consider all that Google does, how can I say that it is evil? Because it is not doing everything that it could reasonably be doing to address the problem.

First, it's important to point out that Google has an inherent conflict of interest. It takes money from people placing ads, and then pays money out to people willing to serve ads. But, for a single click, Google will clearly charge more to place the ad than it will give out to the person serving up the same ad, and the more clicks on an ad, the more Google can charge for the search term in question.

Therefore, in the short term, at least, Google makes more money if there is click fraud.

In the long term, if other ad networks can provide advertisers a better return on the money they spend, it would end up hurting Google. But, right now, Google has a huge stranglehold on the market because it pays more money to legitimate website owners than the alternatives.

Next, if we look at the click fraud Google claims to find versus the click fraud that independent third parties claim is out there, it's clear that there's probably more click fraud going on than Google is actually finding.

Particularly, while Google won't give specific numbers, it claims that "less than 10%" of clicks are fraudulent, and that it consistently catches 98.8% of these clicks before anybody gets charged.

On the other hand, independent evaluators consistently put the number of fraudulent clicks that users pay for well above 10%. For instance, in a study done at the end of 2007, ClickForensics concluded that 28.1% of ad clicks in provider networks were fraudulent and that 16.2% of clicks that people paid for were fraudulent (meaning that Google and similar networks didn't credit the advertiser for that many). To hear ClickForensics tell it, the problem is a heck of a lot bigger than when you hear Google tell it. Google makes it sound like it has the problem under control, but ClickForensics and other companies make it sound like Google is half-assing it.

You can debate the relative merits of how Google and Click-Forensics measure fraud. ClickForensics only studies a sampling of traffic, but it sees broader web usage than Google, which focuses on data it gathers itself.

The truth undoubtedly lies somewhere in the middle, but my own experience in seeing malware perpetrating click fraud leads me to believe ClickForensics is a lot more accurate than Google.

Google has gone out of its way to avoid going into any great depth about click fraud numbers. In one case, instead of letting a class-action lawsuit go to court—where it's widely believed that there would have been plenty of evidence to show big fraud problems—Google quickly moved to settle, paying $90 million instead of fighting it.

No matter what the scope of the problem, as long as Google pays out on a per-click basis, it is inviting fraud.

To be fair, there are worse ways to handle advertising. Instead of paying per click, advertisers can pay per "impression," meaning they pay for each ad that is shown. Clearly, the bad guy doesn't even have to worry much about the clicking in this case (except that without some clicking, the fraud will be pretty obvious).

On the other hand, there is a way to handle advertising even more fairly. Instead of paying sites for displaying ads that are clicked, Google could instead pay the sites for ads that actually lead to a sale. In such a model, Google and the site would take some commission on the sale.

This would be a far more efficient market for advertisers because it virtually eliminates fraud. But, since fraud may constitute a significant part of Google's revenues, especially when you consider how it drives up the cost the company charges for ads, it would probably make far less money in a pay-per-sale model.

Plus, the administrative costs would be higher for Google. It would need to have some confidence that the advertiser is correctly reporting the number and dollar amount of sales. Google could do this by partnering with credit card processing merchants, but then it would have to give up some revenue. Perhaps this is one reason why Google set up its own PayPal-like merchant service, Google Checkout. Even though this service hasn't been a success, Google might eventually come up with an advertising model where pay-per-sale is an option, as long as you use Google Checkout to handle the commerce.

Of course, even though click fraud artificially drives up ad prices, it doesn't totally kill the advertiser, otherwise Google would do more about it. It does help Google drain the advertiser for as much money as feasible.

To some degree, advertisers can adjust for fraud in their planning. They can project how much business they're going to get, as long as there's consistent conversion. If they're not getting a good enough return from their ad campaigns, they just won't advertise anymore.

After all of this, though, who cares about the advertisers? Didn't I say the whole Internet is worse off because of Google, not just people with something to sell?

The consequence of pay-per-click and pay-per-impression models is that the bad guys have far more incentive to break in to machines than they otherwise would. The fewer reasons bad guys have to break in to machines, the less money would be involved, and the less the bad guys would be willing to spend to break in to machines. There would most likely be fewer infections as a result.

There are certainly other reasons for bad guys to infect machines, like those we examined in the previous chapter. And those same reasons would definitely still lead to infections, but if there were no click fraud, the total pot of money for computer crime would be a lot smaller. If the same number of criminals kept trying to make money, nobody would make as much, so plenty of people would move on to other pastures. The costs to break in to a single machine would at least stay the same, and might even go up a bit, because there would probably be fewer people focusing on this kind of thing. Therefore, it's reasonable to believe that there would be fewer infections.

Whether this turns out to be the case or not, Google certainly isn't the only company culpable. Most other ad networks are in the same boat, though Google is certainly the big gorilla in the online advertising space.

There are other companies you can point fingers at when it comes to bad guys infecting machines. Particularly, you can point at banks, because a lot of the rest of the fraud revolves around them.

Banks don't have any significant incentive to see fraud perpetrated. They tend to bear the cost when fraud does happen, so they care quite a bit about the problem. They are willing to spend to keep malware off machines.

However, they aren't doing the most altruistic thing in terms of keeping PCs free of infections, which would be to group together and disallow e-commerce altogether (or at least require people to call in personal details). Consumers wouldn't stand for this. They would rather take the risk of being infected for the convenience of being able to buy things and do their banking online.

Banks still try to do as much as possible to fight this problem. They tend to be active in encouraging people to run antimalware products. They even arrange for people to get good discounts on major players' products. They try to put other safeguards in place that add more protection, like offering little hardware devices for logging in, sending unique passcodes, and so on. They do lots of monitoring to try to pick out fraudulent uses of credit cards and bank accounts, and tend to freeze them if there is any doubt at all. They try to make it easy for the consumer who cares about security to be secure. But at the same time, they realize that most people want the convenience of less security, so they try not to force security measures down people's throats; if something is intrusive, they know their customers will take their business elsewhere.

That's not to say that banks aren't culpable. To me, they just seem less evil. But whenever the desire for bigger profit margins works against the best economic interests of the consumer (especially from a security point of view), there's a bit of evil in this world by my reckoning. That makes banks evil, and it sure makes Google evil.

Really, this tradeoff is an inherent tension in capitalism. If the evil outweighs the massive good of capitalism, it's the job of governments to step in and regulate things in the best interests of their people.

Now, perhaps there should be some regulation in the online advertising world. At the very least, there should be some transparency to make sure companies that are brokering online ads aren't knowingly allowing fraud. Even if companies like Google can't be an open book (because it would give the bad guys a roadmap for further fraud), they could at least be subject to some very stringent government-led auditing.

I'm sure if click fraud becomes enough of a problem that advertisers complain, they'll either spend a lot less on advertising online or governments *will* eventually step in. That's the great thing about economics: these things will eventually sort themselves out.

So even though Google is evil in the sense that it's looking out for its own financial interests on this matter, it is doing pretty much exactly what I'd be doing if I were Google, and it's doing what its shareholders want it to do. Go, Google! Do your evil!

CHAPTER 8

Why Most AV Doesn't Work (Well)

In this chapter, we are going to take a closer look at the bedrock of the industry—antivirus (AV). I'll focus on why it has a reputation for not working well and why that reputation is well deserved. In the next chapter, we'll look at why AV is slow. Note that many companies have been trying to fix these problems, but for most vendors, the going is slow. I'll talk about the timeline for improvement near the end of this book.

Almost everybody runs AV, or at least they think they do. On Windows, over 90% of all people are running AV, and the number of people who think they are is even higher. It's far more pervasive than any other end user technology, and is far more common in people's lives than the only other security technology with fairly widespread ubiquity—the firewall.

It amazes a lot of people that AV technology is so ubiquitous, because it is so widely reviled. Technical people will often claim that AV doesn't work, and that it causes stability problems. And almost everyone will claim that it slows your machine down.

I can't argue. When I was first at McAfee (I was away from McAfee for a brief period and have since returned), I was responsible for the core AV engine development (not the products that consumed the engine). I inherited it. I learned all about it and I studied all the competitors. There were lots of brilliant people in many AV companies around the globe. Yet, I can say pretty unabashedly that most AV products live up to their bad reputation.

Even McAfee's AV wasn't great when I inherited the technology, although it is improving rapidly to this day. For instance, a recent independent comparative test listed McAfee at the top of the pack for malware detection, which is very believable.

First, let's look at what AV is and how the typical technology works, then we'll look at the huge pit of suck and why those problems are there. I'll defer talking about the way I think things "should" be done until Chapter 39.

You might expect me to first define the word *virus* as a key to understanding AV. But AV technologies typically go beyond viruses, also trying to detect worms, botnet software, trojans, and even spyware, adware, and attack tools—even though it can be a touchy subject as to whether most things in the last three categories are bad. For instance, McAfee (and others) have always detected the program nmap as bad, since it can be used as an attack tool, even though many, many good guys use the tool (it simply helps map out which services are visible on a network—the name comes from "network map"). The logic is basically that the average AV user shouldn't have it on his machine, and having the AV software complain about it isn't going to stop the legitimate practitioner from using the tool. There's merit to both sides here, and in many cases things get marked bad where the decision is quite clearly a gray area.

Anyway, all these terms are irrelevant for the moment. Suffice it to say, there is a ton of bad software that you probably wouldn't want on your machine. The industry often refers to generic *mal*icious soft*ware* as *malware*, and we'll use that term. Spyware and adware are sometimes in a gray area where they aren't intentionally malicious and may not be called malware, but you should get the basic idea. AV software is software that tries to identify malware and either prevent you from installing or running it in the first place, or remove it if it's already installed.

There are two ways in which AV software tends to run: *on-access scanning* and *on-demand scanning*. On-access scanning means that some program is about to run, or some other file is about to get used, and the AV checks it first to see if might be bad. On-demand scanning means that files are being checked even if they're not being used. This generally occurs when you're doing a full system scan, which many AV products do when you boot the machine.

Typically, when a file is scanned and found to be bad, the user is notified and some appropriate action is taken, such as removing the file or (particularly in some enterprises) putting it in a quarantine area where it will not run but somebody can go look at it later.

The AV product running on the desktop usually doesn't intrinsically know too much about what's malware and what isn't. That's the job of what the industry calls *DATs* (data files) or *signature files*. The AV product contains an *engine* that knows how to take a file that you want to scan, then query one or more of these signature files to figure out whether something might be bad. The signature files often also encode information about how to reverse infections, if necessary.

Typically, the AV product goes and grabs new signature files once a day (if you are continually online). Some products check twice a day or even hourly (and McAfee now has real-time updates).

AV engines are typically incredibly generic beasts. They're tuned to do pattern matching on arbitrary file types. They need to understand any file type that might potentially be problematic, which is a huge challenge to do well, especially if you're going to try to detect arbitrary data files, such as pictures that could attack your machine if loaded into the wrong photo viewer.

As an example of how generic AV engines tend to be, the McAfee AV engine basically implements multiple programming languages. The signature files contain lots of little programs that the AV engine runs every time it looks at a file to determine whether or not that file is bad. One programming language McAfee uses is tuned for quickly identifying patterns in binaries, and the other is tuned for complicated issues that the other language is too simple to deal with, such as repairs. The first language is explicitly designed so that people writing an individual program in it won't accidentally cause your machine to hang. The other should be used sparingly and tested thoroughly before it is deployed to users.

There's usually an extensive operation behind any AV technology. The vendor needs to know enough to be able to say, "Hey, this file is malware," so it either has to have some secret sauce that allows it to determine malware using an algorithm, or it needs to look at individual programs and make a determination.

What typically happens is that vendors look at malware and try to spot patterns, then write signatures that are generic enough to catch as much malware as makes sense, without flagging something as bad that is clearly good.

Vendor employees then analyze files using some automation, but typically also involving manual effort. There has to be a workflow for tracking submissions and communicating with people who submit malware. Once the vendor analyzes the files, it writes a signature, if appropriate. A signature might be generic enough to detect and repair a whole class of bad stuff, or it might just detect a single piece of malware, perhaps without repairing the actual infection.

Once it writes the signatures, the vendor typically needs to test them extensively to ensure that they're not going to cause problems when deployed. The biggest worry is that the signature will declare something as malware that isn't, in which case the signature is said to have given a *false positive*, or to have *falsed*.

The vendor doesn't like false positives, particularly because this stops people from running software they might want to run, potentially even deleting the software. There have been several prominent false positives in the media, but probably the worst incident occurred in March 2006, when McAfee released a signature update that detected Microsoft Excel (among other things) as a virus and deleted it from machines. Every major vendor has similar tales, and most vendors have more recent tales. In the case of McAfee, that incident really helped speed up the company's efforts for a dramatic improvement in its technology.

AV companies spend a lot of resources trying to prevent false positives. They tend to do extensive testing for signatures, including running them over massive databases of known good programs to make sure that none of those programs get flagged. And in most companies, multiple people review each signature to make sure it won't have a negative impact. Yet false positives still happen, and pretty frequently (though usually on applications that aren't commonly used).

After testing, the AV company can publish the signatures. The publishing process can be complicated, but it's often the case that signatures are published at approximately the same time every day.

The desktop AV client tries to download those signatures when it thinks they might be published, and keeps trying fairly frequently if something is wrong (for instance, the computer might not be online or the signatures might be late in being published).

The AV industry has been working more or less this way for the past 20 years or so. Technologies haven't really improved very much, and they aren't as effective as they should be. Let's look at the problems.

The most obvious problem is scalability. Thousands of new pieces of malware come out every day. These days, most of them are showing up on a fairly small number of computers (say, dozens) before they are automatically "mutated" into slightly different programs that do the same thing. AV companies tend to have up to 100 people working full time on the problem, but each one of those people isn't likely to be able to handle more than a few pieces of malware a day.

Getting lots of people with the right skills to understand and detect malware is extremely challenging, particularly because of the vast technical expertise necessary to figure out what things the clever bad guys have done to thwart the security industry from doing its job.

Not having enough people to handle the flood of malware is a primary reason why detection rates for AV technology are so low (some people say as low as 30% in practice). The industry tries to deal with this by writing signatures for individual pieces of malware, then trying to write signatures that are generic enough to detect as much malware as possible. But the bad guys have gotten pretty good at making this more difficult.

In practice, the better detection tends to come in waves, as the good guys at an AV company work hard to analyze trends over a large number of pieces of malware and write code to generically detect as much as it can. Unfortunately, it doesn't come fast enough, and tends to leave people unprotected from individual threats for long periods of time.

There are a lot of other reasons why there is a long delay in detection (a big *window of vulnerability*). One reason is that AV vendors typically don't get to see enough bad stuff. They use a few methods to get their malware:

- Many vendors swap malware with one another on a daily basis.

- Many vendors have their own systems to crawl around the dark corners of the Internet looking for malware, and leave vulnerable systems around hoping people will break in and leave malware.

- For the largest vendors, the biggest source of malware comes from the customer base. Customers send the vendor malware that the product didn't detect. These are often large corporate customers, not individuals, and in fact, you can bet the large companies get more attention to their problems than the little guys do.

This may all sound well and good, but while this strategy worked well a decade ago (when a single piece of malware tended to infect thousands of users), it doesn't work well now that there are tons more pieces of malware, infecting only a few dozen users at a time.

Another reason for there being a big window of vulnerability is that AV vendors don't want to mess up by having their technology give false positives, like the Microsoft Excel problem we discussed earlier.

But, as I've said, false positives are easy to create. Since AV signature files are code, and it's easy to add errors to code, it stands to reason that it is easy to end up with false positives. To combat that problem, AV companies have to do testing, which takes time. When you combine that with delivering signatures on a daily basis, it's reasonable to expect a 24- to 48-hour lag time between when a piece of malware starts to spread and when an AV product detects it.

In reality, though, it is more like one to three weeks, on average. For example, in 2007, the Yankee Group published a report that discussed a virus known as the Hearse rootkit. A company called Prevx found this rootkit and offered protection more or less immediately. It took McAfee 10 more days to get out a signature, and it took Symantec 13 days.

A lot of people think that a problem with AV technology is that it is a simple pattern-matching utility dressed up to look like something more powerful. That might have been true in some cases at some points, but that's certainly not the case today. Since AV engines tend to have real programming languages in them, they can do arbitrary things.

Just because signature writers can do almost anything doesn't mean they do. Usually, brand-new approaches that could make a major difference aren't easy to build using the technology that already exists in AV products, and new technologies could easily have a significant impact to end users because there would inevitably be lots of bugs and performance issues.

So, as a result, AV companies tend to do four things in their signature files (and often some of this gets pushed into the "engine"):

- Simple pattern matching for individual applications. This often amounts to, "If the file is identical to this piece of malware we saw before, then it is bad." There are some technical tricks to this, but it is effectively looking for an exact match without having to include the entire file for each piece of malware.

- Simple pattern matching for a group of similar applications. This is known as "generic" detection, the hope being that the pattern uniquely identifies a class of malware, and not any legitimate software. With luck, it will help prevent AV companies from having to write lots of individual signatures for other pieces of malware in the family. In some cases, this detection type may hit only one file, but that's rarely the intent these days, since simple signatures do the same thing and don't risk accidentally flagging a good file as bad.

- Look at outside factors (such as possibly suspect behaviors when the software runs) to guess whether it is malware. This is called *heuristic detection*, meaning that the code is taking a best guess, even though the AV company probably hasn't seen that particular program before. This is an area where the biggest AV companies tread very carefully, because if they mess up, they will end up upsetting customers with false positives.

- Attempt to repair the system from an infection.

None of these types of signature content go far enough in addressing the underlying scale problem, though. Addressing the scaling issues would require a significantly different approach. Certainly, AV companies have been trying new things to do better, but it's a slow, experimental process.

Another fundamental problem with AV accuracy is that the bad guys can run AV products, too. Let's say Evil Bill writes a bad piece of software. AV products might detect it out of the gate, but Bill will learn that right away just by running them. He can keep tweaking his malware until the programs stop complaining, then unleash it on the world and be guaranteed some time before anybody stops it (as we've seen, it can easily be weeks).

Making it worse, if Evil Bill does manage to get his malware on your machine, it is hard to recover from it. Bill's software will almost certainly disable your AV software, rendering it inoperable.

These problems seem insurmountable, but some technologies actually hold some promise for addressing most of these issues cost-effectively. The question is, why aren't we already using better technologies?

Most existing AV technologies are about 20 years old. They worked well enough for most of that time to achieve and maintain almost 100% market penetration. So, in a sense, as long as the money keeps flowing in, there isn't a huge economic incentive for big companies that already invested a lot in building their technology to invest a lot more to reinvent it.

Instead, money for new development tends to go to new product lines that can potentially earn more money. For the big guys, it can easily make more economic sense to let someone else (say, a startup) go off and build better technology, and then to acquire it when it becomes necessary.

In the long run, there are technologies that show a lot of promise (such as *collective intelligence* technology, which I will discuss in Chapter 39). These technologies could make the AV company's job a lot easier, but it takes a big investment of time and money to get there. I see the industry starting to move in that direction, but it's still going to be a while before we get there.

CHAPTER 9

Why AV Is Often Slow

OK, so AV typically doesn't do a good job of finding stuff. Now we understand a bit of why that is. But even a bad AV technology can be valuable, because protection against, say, 30% of all threats is still a lot better than protection against 0% of all threats. However, besides the lousy protection, there's still plenty not to like about old-school AV technology.

The average person may not know whether AV software really protects her or not, but she generally knows that it is slow. This is certainly the most common complaint I hear about the technology from average consumers.

So why is most AV so slow? Let's start by looking at the time people notice it most—when their computers are starting up. Yes, any software that's going to protect you proactively needs to load up when the computer starts, and that could take a bit of time. But AV products seem to feel the need to check the files on your computer for signs of bad stuff, and that is often what takes up the time.

The idea behind scanning your computer for bad stuff on bootup is that there might be things on your machine that have been newly determined as bad. So, maybe there's a screensaver you downloaded a week ago, but your AV company just decided today that it is bad. Or, in some cases, you might have gotten bad stuff on the computer when the AV software wasn't running. For instance, you might have a dual-boot machine, meaning you have a second operating system on the machine that can write to the same disk drive. Maybe you run Windows and Linux, and down-loaded some Windows virus while running Linux (where you're unlikely to be running AV).

The typical thing for AV software to do is to look at each file on your filesystem, determining whether or not it's bad. With most AV software, that process of judging a single file is stupidly inefficient.

For instance, many vendors rely heavily on a technique called *cryptographic signature matching*, but do so in an unintelligent way. First, let's look at what cryptographic signature matching is. AV vendors would like to do exact matching and say, "This file we're looking at is an exact digital copy of this bad file we saw yesterday." However, they don't want to have to put every piece of malware ever seen on customers' computers—that would take up too much space and would put even more ammunition in the hands of the bad guys.

Instead, they use some cryptography that takes the file as an input and spits out a number that is a fixed size. The interesting thing is that the number that comes out appears to be purely random, but every time they enter the same input, the same output pops out. The numbers that pop out of this algorithm are big numbers—so big that they won't ever see two different inputs that give the same output.

This algorithm lets AV vendors say, "If a file's cryptographic signature is 267,947,292,070,674,700,781,823,225,417,604,638,969, it is bad." Now, they just have to store this number, not the whole file. The bad guy might like to try to produce bad software that gives the same results as popular good software. For instance, he might try to produce software giving the same cryptographic signature as some version of Microsoft Word, hoping that it will make it harder for vendors to come up with a signature, because a cryptographic signature would give lots of false positives. But the cryptography is the special sauce making this impossible. The number that pops out really is about as good as random, so the most plausible thing a bad guy could do here is write lots of new malware until one finally gives the same result as some legitimate file. And, as you might guess, it would take too many tries to be practical, even if all of the bad guys in the world got together to work on the problem.

Now that we understand cryptographic signatures, let's look at how AV vendors can apply them to this problem. What they'd like to do when looking at a file is determine its cryptographic signature, then look up the signature in a database to see if it's bad. And hopefully a database lookup will be blazingly fast. In fact, there are well-known algorithms where this kind of lookup should indeed be essentially instantaneous. The lookup should be a heck of a lot faster than calculating the cryptographic signature.

Let's assume for the moment that that's what actually happens (often it is not). How long does it take to calculate a cryptographic signature? Well, the cost is dominated by the amount of time it takes to read the file off your hard drive. Everything else that happens is almost irrelevant.

The fastest hard drives today can read about 125 megabytes per second. If your AV software is going to scan, say, 40 gigabytes of files, you are going to spend at least 5 minutes of physical time waiting while the disk is busy feeding data to the AV system, in an absolutely ideal world. In the meantime, when other programs try to access the disk, everything slows down. Your other applications wait for a pause in the AV workload, and then there's a performance hit when the disk has to move around for the various applications. If you're doing a whole system scan where you have to do a cryptographic signature of every file, the net result is that you can expect things to go very slowly.

But, for some AV systems, the story is much worse because there's a lot of additional work for every single file that gets scanned. Instead of just being able to ask, "Now that I processed this file, is its signature in the database?" and get an immediate answer, what typically happens is something more like this:

```
I just processed a file.

Its signature is
267,947,292,070,674,700,781,823,225,417,604,638,969.

Let's call that signature S.

Is S equal to 221,813,778,319,841,458,802,559,260,686,979,204,948?

If so, the file is malware.

Is S equal to 251,101,867,517,644,804,202,829,601,749,226,265,414?

If so, the file is malware.

Is S equal to 311,677,264,076,308,212,862,459,632,720,079,837,243?

If so, the file is malware.
```

...

```
Is S equal to 11,701,885,383,227,023,807,765,753,397,431,618,256?

If so, the file is malware.
```

In one of these bad systems, the question is asked once for every piece of malware that has a cryptographic signature. This approach doesn't scale very well to today's malware problem. Let's see why.

There are about 10,000 new pieces of malware created each day (most of them are automatically generated from other pieces of malware, to avoid detection). Let's assume that an AV company can catch them all. Let's also assume that the company has been adding 10,000 signatures a day for only a year. That's 3,650,000 signatures. If it takes a millionth of a second to process one signature (and it probably will take a few millionths), it would take 3.65 seconds to process all those signatures.

In reality, AV companies have other techniques they prefer to use if they don't have to use cryptographic signatures. They'd like to be able to capture as many pieces of malware as they can with a single signature, and since they generally won't see all of the 10,000 new pieces of malware a day, they're going to focus their signature writing on the "most important" pieces of malware. As you'd expect, big companies generally prioritize what their big corporate customers are sending them over stuff they get from smaller companies, and individuals are very likely to be ignored— even the biggest companies have only a few dozen analysts dealing with these kinds of issues at any given time.

With so much malware, cryptographic checksums are a really important technique. It is easy to write one (automated systems in the backend can easily write signatures), and those signatures are easy to eliminate if they turn out to be wrong.

Certainly, if designed properly,[1] cryptographic signatures can improve efficiency. The stupid way in which they tend to be handled is an artifact of the way signatures have been done forever, this notion of one rule following another, following another.

---

[1] For technical people, one should clearly use hash table lookups or a similarly efficient data structure. But many AV systems still use tree-based algorithms, or even linear scans!

It worked well when there were only tens of thousands of pieces of malware in total, but it doesn't anymore.

AV vendors are starting to shift to smarter ways of dealing with cryptographic signatures. But even when they do, they still have all the noncryptographic signatures. Again, with a traditional AV engine, vendors hope their regular signatures will capture most of the bad stuff. So, as there's more bad stuff that avoids AV engines, they'd like to get signatures that will detect lots of pieces of malware, hopefully even stuff that hasn't been created yet.

As long as there's a big focus on traditional signatures for protection, there are going to be many signatures that can take a lot of time to run, even when vendors do a better job with cryptographic signatures.

Another reason why signatures proliferate and performance decreases as malware grows is because AV vendors generally can't easily remove old signatures. Vendors typically don't keep enough data to determine whether old signatures are unnecessary because of new signatures. Nor do they collect enough information to know when a signature can be removed because the malware it caught doesn't circulate anymore. That might sound risky, but there is malware that wouldn't even work if you did manage to get it on your machine, just because of the way systems have evolved since the good old days of the DOS operating system.

Now that we know a bit more about why AV is a dog, the issue becomes what the end user can do about it. You can choose your AV product based on raw performance numbers, but performance isn't everything. And most products perform well enough when only doing on-access scans.

It's on-demand scans that people notice most, and I recommend that people turn this feature off. There's generally no compelling reason to do a scan of your entire system, particularly if it's going to degrade performance. You might worry that you aren't being protected at all, but AV software is most effective running on-access scans, meaning that the AV engine scans files right before you go to use them. Malware can't hurt your system if you don't run it, so who cares if it is lying dormant on your disk?

The only significant benefit of a full system scan is that you can find bad stuff before you accidentally give it to someone else.

However, almost no malware spreads that way these days, and even if it did, one would hope that the person you gave it to was also running some sort of effective host protection. All in all, I don't think this case is worth slowing down your machine more than necessary.

Also, note that these full system scans usually occur at least once a day—whenever the AV system downloads new signatures. Though, for most people who leave their computer on all day, this may not have an impact, because it tends to be in the middle of the night.

Anyway, a lot of these problems stem from the fact that most AV technologies were not built for scale. Scaling host security is a tough problem, one we'll look at in Chapter 39.

CHAPTER 10

Four Minutes to Infection?

In July 2008, a report went around claiming that if you connect an unpatched and unprotected Windows XP machine to the Internet and did nothing else, it would be infected in four minutes, on average. The typical recommendation for preventing this kind of problem is to run a firewall on your network and to install all the latest updates as quickly as possible.

This all sounds scary, but don't worry, that report is total rubbish. It's just garbage used to spread fear, a marketing tool for the organization producing these numbers (in this case, it's SANS, a company that sells security training and certification and puts on security conferences; this kind of press might bolster its reputation and get people to buy its services).

It's true that there are plenty of automated programs randomly scanning the Internet, looking for vulnerable systems to infect. It's not true that you're likely to be infected.

The primary reason why this is utter hogwash is that Windows XP (as of Service Pack 2) already has a firewall that is protecting you. If you install something older than Windows XP SP2 (which came out in late 2004), you would have to worry about whether there was something on the network protecting you. Though, in many cases, there would be, whether you knew it or not.

Your ISP (Internet service provider) might prevent unwanted Internet traffic from getting to your machine. Your wireless router or cable/DSL modem might have a firewall enabled by default. And your router/modem will probably have NAT (network address translation) enabled by default. NAT will protect you from outside threats even if you're running the oldest version of Windows XP, or even Windows 95.

These technologies are protecting you because they keep traffic from the outside world from reaching the software running on your machine. That's software that is potentially vulnerable. A firewall works by acting as sort of a gatekeeper. It selectively chooses which traffic to let through and which not to let through. A firewall sitting in your wireless router or cable/DSL modem will probably have a policy that boils down to this:

> If a new connection request comes from the outside world, deny it. If a new connection request comes from inside the firewall, allow it, along with any traffic in the follow-on conversation.

This means you can make a connection to a web server from your browser, but if your machine happens to have a web server running on it, nobody from the outside world will be able to connect to it.

NAT acts differently, but has the same basic result. Instead of being a filter per se, it allows lots of computers to share a single IP address (which is generally all your ISP is going to give you). That address usually doesn't allow any inbound connections. It can, but you would have to configure them manually. Instead, everyone inside the network gets an address that doesn't work on the Internet, only on a local network. The NAT device takes outbound connection requests, makes it look like it's coming from the IP address your ISP provides, then takes the data that comes back, and forwards it to whichever machine initiated the connection.

These technologies make it extremely difficult for someone from the outside world to break in to your machine without you doing anything. You generally have to do something that results in your infection. It could be that you go to a website that takes advantage of a security flaw in your web browser or tricks you into downloading something bad. It could be that you get an email message that takes advantage of a security flaw in your email reader, or simply tricks you into installing it. Either way, you are responsible for initiating the outbound connection in the first place (even if your email reader is periodically making that connection on your behalf).

The Windows firewall performs a similar role as a network firewall, but resides on your individual machine instead of on a cable modem or DSL router. That's particularly useful on a large corporate network, where someone else might have gotten infected, and that infected machine might otherwise have access to some vulnerable software service running on your computer. But there's more of a risk from infection on the local network because people tend to be more liberal in what is allowed on the local network. Automatic communication, file sharing, and printer sharing tools are common, and firewalls usually do not block such things by default.

Clearly, there are a lot of prevention mechanisms that keep your computer safe. Even if it's just on your computer, you're probably in good shape. So why would SANS be saying things that don't seem to be true?

First, SANS is indeed measuring something. It publishes daily numbers (though as of this writing, the data stops at November 16, 2008). The number fluctuates. For example, on November 16, 2008, SANS claimed a Windows machine would last a little under 100 minutes before infection unless some network protection device was used.

SANS does not publish its methodology. My best guess is that it is running a version of Windows XP that predates the 2004 Service Pack 2 release. It wouldn't surprise me that a machine running that software would be in trouble if you put it naked on the Internet.

But while people might offer you sound advice (yes, might as well have a firewall, and *yes*, keep your software up to date, especially the things you use, like your web browser), when they make scary claims, don't believe the hype without hard evidence.

CHAPTER 11

Personal Firewall Problems

In the previous chapter, I argued that the Windows firewall helps keep people pretty safe from Internet threats, especially when the user doesn't do anything risky. In this chapter, I'm going to complain about firewalls—but not just any kind of firewall. I'm going to complain about personal firewalls, which are subtly different from the firewall that comes with Windows and the firewall you might run on a network.

What is a personal firewall? Well, a firewall is supposed to monitor traffic entering or leaving either a network (if the firewall lives on a network) or a machine (if it lives on your machine). It allows or blocks traffic based on a policy.

Typically, operating systems have a built-in firewall that is pretty effective. They stop all traffic coming onto the machine, unless it is in response to something the user did (though you can allow exceptions, for instance, if you want to run your own web server on your machine).

But if network traffic is initiated from your machine, the OS firewall generally won't do anything.

Let's say you've accidentally downloaded a banking trojan, which will monitor all your online banking activity and then secretly send your account information to bad guys on the other side of the world. Since you're infected, your AV already failed to detect the bad software, which will go ahead and collect your information.

But even if your personal data is collected, what if you could keep that data from being sent off to the bad guys? Built-in firewalls like the Windows firewall can't really do that (see "The Limitations of Traditional Firewalls" on page 62 for an explanation).

If you want a firewall to stop bad outbound traffic, you need to give it information about which applications are trying to talk, which is the basic idea behind the personal firewall (sometimes called an *application* firewall).

This could allow you to say, "Only Internet Explorer can talk to things on port 80," or, "Let Skype talk to anything it likes."

Policy management is a huge pain in the neck, though. If you want to stop the rogue trojans doing bad things, you need to start out with a policy that denies everything unless you specifically allow it. Enumerating the applications you use is a lot of work, and it's awful to have to remember to configure your personal firewall every time you install new software that might use the Internet.

The way personal firewalls deal with this problem is to give you pop-up windows that force you to make policy decisions. For example, when you install Skype, you may get a pop up that says, "Do you wish *skype.exe* to access the Internet?" And you will generally tell the firewall to "remember your decision" so you don't get the obnoxious prompt again.

Most users hate lots of prompts. It's made worse by the fact that lots of applications have multiple programs that will be treated separately. For instance, most applications have a main executable that, when it comes time to check for software updates, will run a second program. You need to give that one access separately.

Some applications install lots of separate executables. For example, Apple's iTunes installs dozens of different executables with lots of different functions. If you actually used all the features that come bundled, you might end up getting prompted tons of times.

These prompts are the only way to make a personal firewall work reasonably well, but I'd say they're not reasonable enough. It's not just that dialog boxes are obnoxious. It's that they try to get users to make decisions they're not equipped to make.

What tends to happen is that people will eventually see a program they don't recognize. For instance, you might see a prompt that says, *"GCONSYNC.EXE* would like to use the Internet. Do you wish to allow it?" You might say to yourself, "What the heck is *GCONSYNC.EXE*?!?" and you might choose to disallow it, just in case it is something bad. Well, if you do that, you'll be blocking one of the many iTunes components.

Once you block something you recognize and a program breaks, if you're like most people, you'll assume that every program you don't recognize has a valid purpose, and just start allowing everything.

Sure, some people might hunt down information on each executable they allow, but this would take too much time for the average user.

I just turn my personal firewall off. If I'm going to have to click to allow everything it shows me, why bother with the annoying pop ups? If I did leave it on, I'd probably just feel safer than I really am.

I do think it is possible to have a personal firewall that leaves you alone except in very rare circumstances. Take, for instance, *GCONSYNC.EXE*. This program is *signed* by Apple, meaning we can be confident that it's legitimate. Apple is a reputable vendor, so why should anyone ever prompt? Just let the thing through.

Certainly, not every program is digitally signed—lots of them aren't. We won't worry about the technical details here, but we should expect security vendors to be able to build a big list of good software, using all sorts of techniques. Then only warn us about stuff that might be bad, which should be a very short list.

That might sound like a hopeless task, cataloging all software in the world, but vendors are starting to do it quite successfully. It is now possible to have a personal firewall that doesn't suck, because you almost never have to see it.

If done right, you would just get a notification that a program is getting blocked because it is probably bad. You wouldn't have to do anything unless the system was wrong and you needed to override it.

When that day comes, the technology will be so unobtrusive that it will just be a part of your AV. There will be no need to even think about it as a personal firewall. That's good, because most consumers don't know or don't care what a firewall is, anyway.

Even when that day comes, don't expect the personal firewall to die. AV vendors will keep providing personal firewalls because many of their customers expect to see them.

The Limitations of Traditional Firewalls

When data is sent between two computers on the Internet, the underlying Internet infrastructure needs to know how to get that data back and forth. At the simplest level, this is the same problem that the post office has when routing regular mail. The post office solves its problem by giving you an address. On the Internet, machines have addresses, too. Unlike postal addresses, Internet addresses only make sense to machines (they're just sequences of numbers, for example, 157.166.224.25, which is one address that will get you to cnn.com).

Let's say you want to run an email server and a web server on one computer. When someone else connects, you then need a way to distinguish which service that person wants to access. You do this by adding a *port number*, which is kind of like a post office box (there can be a lot of them, all at the same address). Typically, applications have "standard" ports. For instance, web servers often go on port 80 (port 443 if they are talking securely). But that's just convention—you can put your web server on any port you like, and people can still find it.

A traditional firewall allows you to set policy based on network information, primarily address information (though there are other low-level things you can filter on).

A firewall can easily say, "Don't allow new incoming connections to any port on this machine." That's a simple and effective policy, unless you want to run your own services. If you have to run a web server that's visible to the Internet, you can make an exception for that. You can also configure the firewall to allow access to the web server, but only from machines that are local to you.

While firewalls make it easy to protect yourself from the outside world, you can also use them to block connections that you make, when those connections might be made by malicious software.

For instance, if you know that bad guys store their data on one particular computer (and you know its network address), you can tell your firewall not to allow data to go out to that computer's address. Or if you know that one family of malware sends data to lots of different computers, but always uses port 31337, you can disallow all traffic that is destined for port 31337, no matter which address it was destined for.

Or, more realistically, you might decide that you'll only ever use the Web and email, and that everything else you might ever want to use should be blocked. If that were the case, you could just have your firewall block everything that is not commonly used by email or the Web.

Lots of businesses have configured their firewalls this way, but it turns out not to work very well.

The problem here is that bad guys don't want their stuff to be blocked. What they'll do to keep from being blocked is talk over port 80, so that their traffic looks like web traffic to the firewall.

Even legitimate programs like Skype and online games will often decide to send all their traffic over port 80 so that firewalls don't block them.

This is a sensible strategy for them, because it makes their users' lives easier. Often, users have no way to change the firewall policy (especially at work), and they'll be mad at the software manufacturers, not their employers.

Since bad guys can easily send outbound traffic over web ports that looks just like legitimate web traffic, traditional firewalls are not good for stopping outbound traffic—they're only good at keeping stuff from coming in.

CHAPTER 12

Call It "Antivirus"

When the average user needs to get new security for her computer, she doesn't ask for an "Internet security suite"—she asks for an "antivirus product."

This causes people in the security industry so much indigestion that there aren't enough Tums in the world to ease all the suffering.

But this will never change.

When typical consumers think about security protection for their computers, they might think about lots of different things, depending on their degree of technical sophistication. For example:

- Protection from malicious software (including spyware and adware), whether they downloaded it or it attacked them.
- Filtering out spam (though they also expect their email client to do this).
- Protection against phishing (they may also expect this from their browsers).
- Identity protection—they don't have any particular technology in mind, they just think that their security product should be addressing this.
- Parental controls, to help keep their kids from browsing sites with inappropriate content.

- Website ratings, showing which sites might harm their computers as they browse.
- Personal firewalls, inflicting havoc by blocking outbound traffic.
- Host intrusion prevention, which tries to watch the behavior of programs as they run, hopefully blocking bad stuff just in the nick of time when AV fails.

This technology-driven approach is one way to look at things, but the average consumer doesn't care about technologies. In fact, most of these technologies are a big "WTF"[1] for the average person (and for good reason).

No, consumers care about their problems, not about the shiny technological toys (with apologies to those of us in the industry who are rightfully proud of their cool technologies).

What problems do consumers see?

1. People stealing their personal information. People sure care about their finances, their identities, and so on.

2. Bad people destroying their stuff. Maybe they're afraid of losing their personal files, or they might be worried about bad stuff rendering their computers unusable (this used to be a much bigger problem than it is currently, now that bad stuff tries so hard not to be noticed). People typically see backup solutions as an answer to this problem (though they hope their AV will prevent them from getting to the point of needing this in the first place). This is reasonable, particularly since backup also solves the different problem of the hard drive failing (destructive, but not malicious).

3. Spam, spam, spam. It seems to me most consumers will take anything they get for free here, and are probably willing to live with whatever antispam comes with their mail filter.

People would prefer to buy as few products as possible. Ideally, they wouldn't have to buy any, and some people don't (for example, when Apple has convinced them that they don't need to do so).

---

[1] Finally, I found an acronym my copyeditor won't make me spell out on first use!

In a problem-specific view of the world, people will put labels on *solutions to problems*, which is why Marketing calls them *solutions* instead of *technologies*.

For problem #1 (and to some degree, #2), people identify with AV. This is because the masses were educated about the risks of being online over a decade ago, when the risks were called viruses. Now we have dozens of confusing terms for the risks that are out there, including:

- Viruses
- Worms
- Trojans
- Spyware
- Adware
- Rootkits
- Exploits
- Vulnerabilities
- Malware
- Bots/botnets

For about two minutes, the security industry thought that anti-spyware would be a big thing, mainly because the industry saw some technical differences in new bad stuff and released separate products that sold for a little while.

And some people in the corporate world understood the technical difference and wanted to be protected. A few consumers thought, "better safe than sorry," but most people just want to be protected from their problems without having to care anything about the technology. They would get irate with their vendors if there were some threat that their vendor could have protected them from and didn't. And who would want to buy one of each of the following: AV, anti-spyware, anti-trojan, anti-adware, anti-rootkit, anti-exploit, and anti-bot? Even if they all clocked in at the same ultimate price as an all-in-one product, nobody really wants to deal with that complexity.

What people want is to put their trust in one vendor to protect them, and buy, at most, one product to solve what they see as the problem. All of those technical types of bad stuff—who cares? There's just one real problem there; let one product address it.

In any case, if there are companies trying to market multiple products when some other company of similar reputation is trying to sell one product to do the same thing, what's going through the customer's mind? Here's what I would be thinking:

> Clearly, the two companies I trust are likely to be equally on top of things. If one is selling me multiple products, it is probably a moneygrubber, and maybe I should go with the other guy instead.

In effect, consumers expect all protection against bad stuff to be bundled when they buy "antivirus" protection. The term kills people in the industry, especially geeks, because there's a lot more than "antivirus" protection in the products, even though the name makes it sound otherwise. But everyone in the consumer world got used to the notion that "antivirus" is the thing that protects them, without caring about the technical answer to the question, "What is a virus?" And, as you know, the customer is always right. Therefore, to my mind, the answer to, "What is a virus?" is, most properly, "Anything malicious that runs on your computer," because that is the definition 99% of the world has in their heads.

The marketing people don't like this truth, either. They all try to brand their protection suites as "Internet security suites." If you look closely, the core idea behind an Internet security suite is, "This protects you better than just AV." Usually, that's because the vendor threw in all the bells that the user might not need or want, like antispam, child protection controls, and so on. The protection should be about the same.

Not all consumers assume it's the same. Consumers tend to fall into two camps:

- Those who assume the only "good enough" protection is the most expensive version.
- Those who assume the basic version is "good enough" or else it wouldn't be an offering, and everything else is just bells and whistles.

Very rarely do people actually dig down into the details to see what they're buying. It's all "antivirus" to them, *not* Internet security. As a result, even when companies offer four different suites at four different price points, almost every single customer will go for either the cheapest one or the most expensive one.

People do get what you mean if you say "Internet security," but they see that as a more generic term that can apply to the whole industry and any product that comes out of it. They do realize there might be more products. They've maybe heard about firewalls. They know about antispam. And so on. But when it comes time to look for software to keep crap off their computers, they will be thinking, "What antivirus should I get?"

This is the category, no matter what the technology is under the hood. Every few years, someone will claim that "AV is dead" and that their new technology is the future. *Wrong.*

Get in the product mindset, not the technology mindset. Security goobers think, "That old technology sucks," and they consider "antivirus" the old technology. That's not the way the consumers think of it, though. They don't understand the technology, so it must therefore all be AV. It's just that—like in many, many other fields—technologies are improving as time goes on.

If you tried to rebrand the electric car to some totally new name, people would shrug and call it a car, or else they would be confused as to why they would want or need this new thing when they already have a car.

Listen up, all you marketers (and all you venture capitalists) who think your security technology is so awesome: in order to change the name, you have to argue why the technology solves a problem that AV wasn't solving. If it just solves the same problem better, you will never get people to understand why your new term is relevant to them, and therefore it will fail. You are far better off positioning yourselves as "better AV," and then clearly saying why you are better.

For instance, when my last startup was absorbed back up into McAfee, we were about to go to market with a consumer security offering. We were calling it AV, and it was better because:

- Our paid AV product came with an infection-free guarantee— we would clean your computer for free if you did end up infected.

- Our AV protected against new threats—on average, 30 days faster than anybody else.

- Our AV was fast and didn't slow down your machine in the way most other AV solutions are notorious for doing.

- Our AV was cheaper than the major vendors.

This is all well and good. If you think about it, you can assume from this that our technology must be a lot better than "traditional" AV. But what if we decided to invent a new term for it, like a Community Intrusion Prevention System (a term used by another small vendor)? What goes on in the minds of the consumers?

First, they'd be saying, "What the heck is it, and why the heck do I need it?" The answer is, "We're like AV, but better." Now, a company in this position will have to spend a lot of time educating people on why it's not AV, whether or not it's replacing AV (or whether they should have both). It will create confusion, and people don't try too hard to get past that confusion if there's not widespread adoption. They figure that if they need to buy your product, and they don't understand it, they'll just wait until it's proven itself.

"But wait!" the marketing person might say. "Our solution is better!" If you can get people through the confusion of a company positioning against AV without claiming to solve any new problems (only claiming to solve the old problem better), there will probably still be plenty of skepticism. "Can it *really* replace AV? I'll bet it can't. Either it's too new to work well, or it doesn't do the job; otherwise, why wouldn't everyone be using it?"

Even if you claim to have "next generation AV," you still have to convince people of the benefits of your solution. But at least you don't start out by confusing customers.

In short, the security industry should do itself a favor and stop quibbling about terminology. Embrace the term "antivirus." Who cares if it's technically accurate? The customer is always right.

CHAPTER 13

Why Most People Shouldn't Run Intrusion Prevention Systems

The IT security industry is filled with plenty of technologies that work, but don't do enough—technologies that sell, even if they're not particularly cost-effective. One of the most pervasive security technologies that typically isn't cost-effective is the intrusion detection/prevention system. Some vendors might have you believe every company needs this kind of technology, but I'm not so sure. Particularly, I think small companies should be careful to think about whether it is really going to be a cost-effective solution.

The idea behind network-based intrusion detection and intrusion prevention systems (NIDS and NIPS, respectively) sounds pretty appealing. Stick a box on your network that will look at all traffic. The box will do some analysis and tell you when you're being attacked (in the case of a NIDS) or even drop attacker traffic automatically (in the case of a NIPS).

It sounds like a good thing to have all that insight into what's happening on your network, because it's insight that you didn't have before. But turn on your typical intrusion detection system for the first time, and you will get spammed. Intrusion detection systems regularly give off over 10,000 alerts a day.

Clearly, not all of those alerts map to real intrusions, but it's clear that to get value out of an intrusion detection system, you need to be able to separate some of the good alerts from the many irrelevant ones.

Why are intrusion detection devices so spammy? People love to talk about false positives, and certainly there are plenty. However, it's not nearly the whole problem, the way some people think.

What tends to happen is that bad guys are continually crawling the Internet, trying to find issues they can leverage. Yes, the entire Internet is continually under attack. For instance, anybody who runs a server with password authentication enabled will notice a sea of login attempts.[1]

Bad guys really do manage to break in to machines by guessing passwords, so it's certainly not a false positive for an intrusion detection device to report it, but most of these attack attempts are going to fail. Some of them can easily succeed, though, if you've got people with very poor (or blank) passwords. So it doesn't necessarily make sense to ignore everything.

Just because NIDS and NIPS technologies have lots of noise that is not due to false positives, that doesn't mean false positives aren't a problem. They certainly are—common reports are that many devices can be good for thousands of false positives a day. But the point is that even if you can get rid of all the false positives, you don't get rid of the high management costs. Lowering the number of alerts takes a lot of work. You have to understand each class of problem, which takes time.

The whole "tuning" process is this very expensive upfront cost. And, even after tuning, there can be a significant ongoing cost to look at data on alerts that you might want to review. For instance, some people might want to try to correlate failed SSH logins to other network traffic that might indicate a successful intrusion (whether manually or with a security event management product). The upfront costs alone are large enough that it doesn't make much sense for most small and medium businesses to do this kind of thing.

Let's say you're managing a network of 40 users on a corporate DSL line. And let's say you get your NIDS/NIPS and somehow manage to eat the upfront costs, and you tune the system to the point where it is down to just 30 messages a day that you see and

---

[1] My personal SSH server doesn't allow password authentication—this keeps most such attempts away, and yet, yesterday I still got almost 600 attempts.

need to take action on. Let's say that each message takes only 5 minutes to investigate. If your team is spending 2.5 hours a day on the problem, that's going to cost potentially 30K a year in opportunity cost (time where your IT staff could be more productive). Does your team really spend an average of 2.5 hours a week cleaning up infections? And even if it does, is the NIDS/NIPS system actually going to stop you from incurring the cleanup costs or just bring them to the surface faster??

In short, the economics don't look that great for small and even medium businesses. But they do typically make sense in the enterprise. There's more tolerance for the upfront costs, and even the ongoing cost, since having even a half-dozen people spending their days mining intrusion prevention system data could make more sense for monitoring a network of 40,000 users than it does to spend the money for one person to monitor 40 users.

The only way that there's any hope of NIDS/NIPS being cost-effective for small businesses is if they can somehow benefit from scale. This is the entire idea surrounding Managed Security Services (MSS), as offered by such companies as Symantec (through its Riptech acquisition), BT Counterpane, and VeriSign (through its Guardant acquisition). If those guys monitor and analyze data for 40,000+ users, as if they were one big company, they can do the job pretty cheaply. If they had 400 companies with 100 users each, the total cost would be a lot larger because those companies would have no economy of scale. Instead, the one big company could offer the service to the 100-person companies at a lower cost than what they could do it for themselves. They wouldn't have to go through the trouble to get people trained, and they wouldn't have to cover equipment costs, or deal with machines breaking.

But even a managed service costs enough money that it probably isn't right for all companies. If you have your own network servers that are Internet accessible, it might be worth the cost. But if you let someone else host your website and you have no IT other than the desktop machines your employees use, it may not be worth it even to outsource your intrusion detection to a managed service provider.

Instead, you can stick your users behind a NATing router, and then the outside world won't be able to get at your machines unless someone on the network does something to infect your network.

Nobody on the outside can get into the network unless they're invited in. And traditional AV should be at least as good at catching early threats as an intrusion detection device. Sure, you can still do intrusion monitoring, but since there's nothing the bad guy can see (until your users connect to the bad guys or open some attachment from one of them), it's generally more cost-effective to go spend your security budget on other things.

Having run small businesses, I would be very wary of spending anything on intrusion monitoring products or services before I see a real cost benefit—I would need to be spending enough in dealing with intrusions that demonstrably could have been prevented to make the expense worthwhile.

If you do have the need for services that usually are met through dedicated server IT (such as mail servers and websites), you can always control those costs by pushing them off to someone else to manage. Why pay for running and administering your own web servers (it's much cheaper to secure a cluster of machines dedicated to offering only a single service, by the way) when you can just host your content and let someone else deal with the security problem?

If the answer is that you have lots of backend application stuff, then instead of hosting content in the cloud, why not host your applications in the cloud? Let Amazon or Google handle the security. Of course, you have to trust them to do a good job here, but the big guys can generally show their methods and their success at protecting the infrastructure they manage.

For small and medium businesses, this tends to be an excellent solution, because cloud-based computing has all the scale advantages that make it cheap for the small guy. There does come a point where you have enough scale that it's worth doing yourself, but that doesn't apply to too many people.

In summary, NIDS/NIPS is good for the big guys, but tends to be way too noisy to be cost-effective for everybody else. Managed services can help make it cost-effective for medium-size shops, but effective NIPS, even if managed, requires not just the infrastructure, but also an ongoing investment of money and time—two things that small guys usually lack.

And they have better alternatives, like the cloud, or simply going without, incurring cost on an as-needed basis.

CHAPTER 14

Problems with Host Intrusion Prevention

The basic idea behind HIPS (host intrusion prevention system) technology is that it tries to protect you where traditional signature-based AV fails, primarily by watching the behavior of programs that your AV allows to run. If it sees a program behaving badly, the HIPS will stop it (hopefully before it does anything too bad).

I previously argued that in the consumer's mind, it's all AV; this is just some other arcane thing that's trying to keep the bad stuff off. Who cares what it does?

If you do care, the distinction HIPS vendors used to make was that AV is all signature matching—that people write signatures, and those get sent down to end users. HIPS, they would say, is proactive, not reactive. It detects based on bad behavior and will hopefully detect new things, where the AV products don't have signatures.

Bah, humbug!

AV products, almost without exception, have HIPS technology in them. It might be called "heuristic detection" or something innocuous like that, but it's in there!

Now, standalone HIPS products generally do more proactive detection than the typical AV product, but that's because the typical HIPS product will give way too many false positives.

People don't like to be annoyed by pop ups, especially from software they bought that's supposed to make their lives better.

HIPS technology that doesn't generate false positives a lot goes into AV products. Any other HIPS technology should never run in an environment where people might install lots of different kinds of software.

Plus, HIPS turned out not to be very proactive after all. Looking at behavior doesn't solve any of AV's biggest problems. Particularly, HIPS vendors might imply that they solve what I'll call "the testing problem," but they absolutely do not.

What's the testing problem? If a bad guy wants to infect people with malware without being caught by the major vendors, he buys all their products and keeps testing and tweaking his malware until nobody detects it anymore. If a bad guy can do this, he has probably bought himself at least a month before all the major AV vendors are detecting him, and potentially a lot longer than that.

That same testing works against behavior blocking technologies.

You might think, "Can't the HIPS technology just specify all possible bad behaviors?"

Unfortunately, the answer is (for all practical purposes), "No, not without false positives" (blocking programs people may legitimately want to run). For example, you might have a behavioral rule that says, "If a program is capturing keystrokes that are intended for some other program, block it." This rule will stop keyloggers (programs that read and record key strokes) that are trying to grab your credit card data. It will also stop legitimate programs that want to give their expert users the capability to do things in their applications without bringing up the window.

What programs might want to do that?! Skype, for one. I was surprised when I learned this, but Skype seems to have some worthwhile reason for doing this, and it's not the only legitimate vendor that does this kind of thing.

Here's a slightly more complicated example. Let's say there's a program (*IsItBad.exe*) that has the following behaviors:

1. It writes a lot of crap out to disk, including images, data files, and one or more executables.

2. Those executables start decrypting themselves when they run.

Someone in the security industry might think, "That's probably a 'dropper' installing malware." And, statistically, there would be a very good chance that was right, and you could have a HIPS rule to block based on this behavior.

However, *IsItBad.exe* might also be a game that installs a bunch of crap, and that crap is encrypted because the game designers don't want people to have an easy time getting at their intellectual property.

Of course, we should be able to define behaviors that no legitimate software should ever use. We have to be careful, though, because we can easily be surprised by what legitimate programs can do (again, think of the Skype example).

The problem is that as we build more behavioral-based rules, bad stuff will try to look as much like legitimate software as possible. There are always going to be behavioral gray areas where it can't be clear to a security technology running on a single machine whether or not a program is bad. It will require some sort of human insight to make that judgment.

In fact, some things that security researchers might label spyware can easily fall into a gray area where reasonable people can disagree on whether it is bad.

For example, if you didn't read the fine print of the EULA (end user license agreement) of some software you were installing, and the software is serving you up ads that you didn't expect (even though it was explicitly mentioned in the EULA), is that bad? Some people might say it is outright adware. Everyone would think it's bad if it spams you with hundreds of ads. But the less intrusive the ads are, the less clear it is that something is truly bad.

We can't expect a piece of security software to always get the "right" answer when there sometimes *isn't* a right answer.

Another thing HIPS is supposed to do that traditional AV didn't is to provide protection when legitimate applications have security flaws the bad guys can attack. Some AV products include those features of HIPS to the degree that it makes sense. (Besides false positive risks here, which are far larger than just trying to separate good programs from bad, this kind of technology tends to have a significantly negative impact on performance.)

As I've said, the HIPS technology that works without false positives just got moved into AV products because it's addressing the same problems and fundamentally overlaps "traditional" AV. That is, the technologies do protect against a lot of the same things, but they each have value that the other doesn't (even if that value is all technical, in the realm of stuff that few people should even want to care about).

But there are places where people may not care as much about the false positives. For example, large companies might consider running HIPS on their servers if the software on those servers doesn't often change.

The theory goes that you can run the HIPS product in *monitoring mode* for a few months on your production servers to see what kinds of false positives might crop up. You then tell the HIPS product to never show you any of those alerts again. Then you set it to block anytime some future alert pops up.

This can work, but there are challenges that companies should be prepared to face. One challenge is that this "training" phase can be too expensive, and it needs to be done every time you install a new version of the software (for instance, to a more secure or more feature-rich version). Plus, some technologies may still have a high risk of false positives, even after a few months of operation.

CHAPTER 15

Plenty of Phish in the Sea

Phishing (attempting to steal passwords or other sensitive information by posing as a trustworthy website) is one of the biggest concerns in the security industry today. It's a problem that many security technologies are trying to solve, and it's getting a lot of press by banks, particularly ones that are frequent targets of these attacks. Frankly, that's most banks these days.

Certainly, the impression we're supposed to get is that phishing is easy money and people are getting rich. But an interesting report[1] came out recently that argues why that isn't the case.

The authors of that report cleverly compare phishing to traditional fishing (yes, with an "f" instead of a "ph"). As you get more fishermen, there are fewer fish to catch, and the fishermen have to work harder to catch the same number of fish (usually they go farther out to sea and work longer).

In the phishing world, it's the same, except there's only one kind of phish to catch (let's call the breed "suckerphish"). The pool of potential phishing victims doesn't grow very fast. And, once people have been phished, not too many of them get thrown back into the pond (meaning that people who have been phished before are generally more wary and less likely to be phished again).

---

[1] *http://research.microsoft.com/en-us/um/people/cormac/papers/phishingastragedy.pdf*

If there are lots of bad guys phishing, it's problematic for all the bad guys. They have to try harder to find victims, meaning far more phishing attempts, and the bad guys are each going to make less money (on average).

It's not too surprising that the bad guys are in this situation, because it is exceptionally easy to phish. It doesn't take much technical skill to make an email message or a website that looks legitimate.

The good guys, in the meantime, are particularly worried about the problem because there are so many phishing attempts made. The good guys believe there's a big problem and that the losses are huge. So, they've tried all sorts of things in hopes that you'll be able to tell when you're being phished and when you aren't.

For instance:

- Most email messages from people who legitimately have your financial information (banks, PayPal, etc.) will include things that a bad guy isn't likely to have, like the last four digits of your account number.

- When you go to legitimate websites, most of them will have some sort of in-browser mechanism to try to help build your confidence in the site. For instance, Bank of America is known for its SiteKey technology, which requires you to recognize a picture when you are logging in to the website. This is not foolproof, however.

- Some financial sites have optional physical authentication mechanisms, usually for their most paranoid customers. For instance, E*Trade users (and others) can get a physical device that generates one-time numbers. The user has to put in the same number that's showing on the device at that moment. In a slightly different scheme, Bank of America (and other banks) will let you enroll in a system where you have to type in a one-time password each time, which they send as a text message to your phone.

These technologies aren't perfect, often because they rely on the end user being savvy. However, they do raise the bar, making it even harder on the phishers.

Taking the economics to their conclusion, the average phisherman probably makes very little. The study mentioned earlier argued that the average phisherman is making less than he could be making with other career opportunities that are available to him. However, I'm not certain that's true. Many people who get into phishing live in areas that are severely depressed. There may be few other jobs locally available, and they would pay whatever the local economy would bear. If people can phish money from Americans, even if they are making well below the U.S. minimum wage, they could easily be making far more than they could make at an unskilled job (if they could get one).

Whatever the case, as time goes on, phishers should expect to make less and less money. Those who make a good living at it will be those who are able to come up with new phishing techniques that trick people who are otherwise hardened to phishing attempts.

For instance, despite having great security practices and a great security team, Amazon.com is, for the moment, a pretty juicy target for phishers, for the following reasons:

- Most Amazon.com customers get a lot of ad email messages from the site.

- The email recipients have no obvious way to authenticate that the email message came from Amazon.com (see Figure 15-1). The email message is sent in HTML (meaning it's a web page, and most mail readers will show it like a web page). To verify the site's authenticity, you basically need to examine the links and make sure they lead to the right places. Usually you can hover the mouse over the link to see the destination, but few people do this.

- Nobody is used to getting Amazon.com phishing email messages (because phishers aren't targeting it much, if at all).

- Nobody expects that it would be a valuable phishing target, because you can't directly get financial information.

- Amazon.com does force you to type your password a lot, so a phishing email message that leads you to a site that looks exactly like Amazon.com and asks for your password isn't going to be too suspicious.

Figure 15-1. Amazon frequently sends ads to its customers, such as this one

What value is a phished Amazon.com account? If I were the bad guy, I'd do the following:

1. Get a domain name or two that won't arouse too much suspicion. That means it should have "amazon" in it—maybe www1-amazon.com or revalidation-amazon.com.

2. Send out email messages that look like they legitimately come from Amazon.com, advertising something new that people could actually buy there. The email message should just be an ad, and not indicate "something is wrong," like most phishing email messages do. "Something is wrong" + no specific account info = obvious phishing attempt.

3. When the victim clicks on a link in the email message, send her to a page that is exactly like the Amazon.com login page, with the email address filled in, but with the password left blank (as a bad guy, you definitely don't know it).

4. Once the user types in the password and clicks the button, try to log her into Amazon.com. If the password she enters is wrong, show her the same screen Amazon.com would have shown if she was logging in directly.

5. Send her whatever pages Amazon.com sends you. Sit in the middle of their conversation, but let the user do whatever she wants on Amazon.com. That is, she sends the information to you, then you forward it to Amazon, and then show her whatever web pages Amazon wants her to see.

6. Log everything in case the user happens to enter credit card information.

7. After a few days, I'd start logging into Amazon.com accounts for which I've got the login info (this would all be automated). I'd start looking for recently placed orders that aren't going to ship for a day or two (so Amazon.com won't be sending legitimate email messages for a little while).

8. I'd then send an email message that looks exactly like the message Amazon.com sends when your credit card didn't work and you need to fill in new info (see Figure 15-2).

9. When the user clicks the link, she goes to the bad guy site again. This time it's a bit more tricky, but basically I would make it look like I was Amazon.com, capturing her new credit card info for the order in question, but otherwise showing her what she'd be seeing if she was on the real Amazon.com.

Recently, my bank changed out my check card because it had had a big breach, so something I ordered on Amazon.com didn't go through. Amazon.com sent me the email message you see in Figure 15-2.

The message was all text, but a bad guy would have to make it HTML so that the links would look like they point to Amazon.com, when they actually point to the attacker's site.

From: "Amazon.com Customer Service" <payments-update@amazon.com>
Subject: **Important Notice: Your Amazon Order # 102-1729097-9127453**
Date: November 10, 2008 3:18:22 AM EST
To: "viega-amazon@zork.org" <viega-amazon@zork.org>
Cc: "payments-mail@amazon.com" <payments-mail@amazon.com>

Regarding Order 102-1729097-9127453 from Amazon.com

1 of Absolute Sandman Vol. 04
1 of Entropy in the UK (The Invisibles, Book 3)
1 of The Invisibles Vol. 1: Say You Want a Revolution
1 of The Absolute Sandman, Vol. 3
1 of The Absolute Sandman, Vol. 2
1 of Bloody Hell in America (The Invisibles, Book 4)
1 of Counting to None (The Invisibles, Book 5)
1 of Apocalipstick (The Invisibles, Book 2)
1 of The Invisible Kingdom (The Invisibles, Book 7)

Greetings from Amazon.com,

Your credit card payment for the above transaction could not be completed.
An issuing bank will often decline an attempt to charge a credit card if
the name, expiration date, or ZIP Code you entered at Amazon.com does not
exactly match the bank's information.

Valid payment information must be received within 3 days, otherwise your
order will be canceled.

Once you have confirmed your account information with your issuing bank,
please follow the link below to resubmit your payment.

We recommend you select an option to create a new payment method when
prompted and enter the complete information for the payment method you
wish to use.

http://www.amazon.com//gp/css/summary/edit.html/?orderID=102-1729097-9127453

To view your transaction status online, please visit:

http://www.amazon.com/gp/css/history/view.html

We hope that you are able to resolve this issue promptly.

Please note: This e-mail was sent from a notification-only address that
cannot accept incoming e-mail. Please do not reply to this message.

Thank you for shopping at Amazon.com.

Amazon.com Customer Service
http://www.amazon.com

Figure 15-2. *A legitimate message from Amazon.com indicating that a credit card payment did not go through*

In the grand scheme of things, making all of this happen with a minimum of human involvement isn't a huge investment of time. Someone with enough technical skill could easily knock it all out in a week. A more professional criminal would probably take more time with it to make sure it all works right and to tie it into a botnet infrastructure to make it harder for the good guys to take down the attack once they realize what's going on (in this case, the bad guy would move the bad web server around from hacked machine to hacked machine).

This doesn't say anything bad about Amazon. As I said previously, I do know that it has a great security program. I only use it as an example because I'm a loyal customer and know it very well. The real lesson is that there are going to be many non-obvious ways for bad guys to make money from phishing, and so the pool of potential "phish" is nowhere near exhausted.

Right now, there's basically a huge lake full of phish to catch, and nobody else is phishing there. So, somebody can make a lot of money, but it will be easy to overphish.

Once people are hit by our example phishing attack, awareness will start going up, especially as the number of attempts on Amazon.com goes up. Amazon.com will likely implement some measure to try to make it clear that its email messages are legitimate (like an obvious header that contains your real name, which you hopefully will notice if it's ever missing). As a result, this attack will eventually stop working well. People will get very suspicious about Amazon.com email messages and will only browse directly to Amazon.com instead of clicking on links in the email messages. Or, so we should hope.

But it's not right to say that there's no money to be made in phishing (or fishing, for that matter). There are still plenty of opportunities like this, where technologically innovative bad guys can make some money.

CHAPTER 16

The Cult of Schneier

There's no doubt that the world's leading IT security expert is Bruce Schneier. Sure, Bruce Schneier may not be a household name, but he's certainly far better known than anyone else in the field.

Bruce definitely deserves the recognition. He's been, by far, the most prolific security pundit out there since he started his Crypto-Gram mailing list in 1998, which he has since supplemented with a very popular blog. He's written some great books on the security industry that are accessible to a mass market (meaning normal people can easily read them), such as *Secrets and Lies* (John Wiley & Sons). He comments on most things that happen in the IT security field, and he's usually spot on—over the years, there have only been a few issues on which I've personally disagreed with his stance.

Bruce has had rock star status among geeks ever since he wrote *Applied Cryptography* (John Wiley & Sons), which is still one of the best-selling IT books out there. Undoubtedly, it is the #1 IT security book of all time. Even though the second edition of the book came out in 1996 and it hasn't been updated since, it is still in print, and still a strong seller.

Personally, I'm quite grateful to Bruce. I believe the foreword he wrote for my first book in early 2001 (*Building Secure Software*, coauthored with Gary McGraw; Addison-Wesley) helped bring a lot of attention to us, the book, and maybe even the fledgling software security space (which really was only the bugtraq mailing list at the time).

Because Bruce is the most quoted expert in the space and has been so right so often, and because lots of geeks thought *Applied Cryptography* was so cool (many call it the "crypto bible"), geeks usually treat him with reverence. If Bruce issues an opinion, you'd think that Moses had brought down another commandment off Mt. Sinai.

Though I'd like to see more people thinking for themselves, I suppose there's not much wrong with joining the Cult of Schneier, putting the guy on a pedestal, and assuming all of his opinions on security matters are valid. Like I said, he's earned his reputation as IT security's top pundit.

However, like any good religion based on written texts, there are differences in interpreting the holy word.

After many years of evaluating the security of software systems, I can firmly state that I'm against people using the book that made Bruce famous when they're designing the cryptographic aspects of a system. In fact, I can safely say that even though that book is the primary source people use for crypto design, I have never seen a secure system come out the other end. And I don't mean that people forget about the buffer overflows. I mean the crypto is crappy.

My rule for software development teams is simple: don't use *Applied Cryptography* in your system design. It's fine and fun to read it, just don't build from it.

Orthodox members of the Cult of Schneier take this rule as heresy. By orthodox, I mean the generally accepted, most popular belief. But in the introduction to Bruce Schneier's book *Practical Cryptography*, he himself says that the world is filled with broken systems built from his earlier book. In fact, he wrote *Practical Cryptography* in hopes of rectifying the problem.

So, even though I'm in the minority of Schneierists, I think my position is well supported by scripture.

I'm sure there are many brainwashed orthodox cult members out there who are wondering how this could be possible.

Giving Bruce's book to a developer is like giving an average adult a huge toolbox with a large variety of tools, along with an instruction manual for everything in the tool box, and then having him build a house. He gets many varieties of hammers, screwdrivers, and so on. He gets lots of different types of nails and screws. He gets detailed information about how to use all the pieces. But there's no overall guidance on homebuilding. How do you make a roof that doesn't leak? How do you put in windows and doors and do all the insulation? The toolbox and manual are probably enough so that a person could actually build something that resembles a house, but it is almost certainly not going to be of high enough quality to keep out the rain and elements in the way we would typically expect.

In a similar vein, Schneier's book talks about the fundamental building blocks of cryptography, but there is no guidance on putting together all the pieces to create a secure, authenticated connection between two parties.

Plus, in the nearly 13 years since the book was last revised, our understanding of cryptography has changed greatly. There are things in the book that were thought to be true at the time that later turned out to be false. For instance (pardon me while I slip into techno-babble; the terms aren't important to the point), MD5 was considered very strong at the time, but is now known to be insecure for many uses. Also, the book recommends that, for message integrity, you use CBC (cipher-block chaining) mode and use a noncryptographic checksum over the plain text as the last block of plain text. Even though it was presumed secure at the time, this is now known to be insecure.

Because of that 13-year gap, there are also lots of things that a developer should know about that weren't mentioned back then. For instance, there is nothing on the SSL/TLS (Transport Layer Security) protocol or the HTTPS (HTTP over SSL) protocol. Any good book covering how to build a practical secure system easily should cover how to use these things correctly (hint: it's not as easy as it sounds).

For those who are interested in crypto gobbledygook, what set me off on this rant was seeing yet another system that encrypts without message authentication. The system authors were proud that they were using the CBC encryption mode instead of ECB (electronic codebook) mode, because there would have been easy attacks against ECB mode. However, there are easy attacks against CBC mode, too, when (as is almost always the case) you care about your message staying intact. *Applied Cryptography* predates work on encryption modes that offer both confidentiality and message authentication by several years, and predates NIST (National Institute for Standards in Technology) standards for CCM (CBC+CTR mode) and GCM (Galois-Counter Mode) by about a decade. And even if a developer does pick one of these superior modes, it's very easy to use them incorrectly.

I'd like to make a plea for Schneierists to not accept every word Bruce Schneier has written as utterly factual (even though he does totally rock). Maybe, once in a very long while, the guy can be expressing an opinion! Or maybe he might even be wrong every decade or so. And, most importantly, if he's right today, it doesn't always make him right tomorrow.

CHAPTER 17

Helping Others Stay Safe on the Internet

My nontechnical acquaintances often ask me how to stay safe on the Internet. If you're reading this, you probably have developed a pretty good intuitive sense of what you should or shouldn't do. But what about your friends and family, who aren't as well informed and technical as you?

Here's some advice you can give them:

- When your computer wants to install updates for the operating system, for your web browser, or for anything else that you use to connect to random sites on the Internet, do it as soon as possible! This is important because bad guys can use software flaws to take over your computer without you knowing it, using flaws in the software you run.

- Don't use software you download from a file sharing application (e.g., Limewire, Kazaa, Bearshare, or any other program that allows you to download music or programs off the Internet). Often, such software has malware.

- Don't click on ads unless you are already very familiar with the company or product. "Fun" looking ads, or ads that seem too good to be true (e.g., win a free iPod), are almost always scams, and very occasionally will automatically download bad stuff to your computer.

- Try to avoid giving out your personal information unless you're sure the vendor is legitimate. A good free tool to help you figure out which sites are legitimate is SiteAdvisor (*www.siteadvisor.com*). It shows you red, yellow, and green for each site as you browse.

- Don't open email attachments from people you don't know.

- Only open email attachments if you're sure they were intentionally sent to you (viruses will sometimes email themselves out).

- Run AV and make sure your subscription doesn't expire.

- Lots of websites that distribute software bundle bad stuff with their downloads. Also, some software that appears legitimate turns out to be bad. Only install software if:

  - A reputable source determines that it is spyware-free. Specifically, if you find it on download.com, you should see "tested spyware free."

  - A thorough web search turns up no ties to bad stuff. For example, if you're searching for FrobozCo WidgetWare, search for "FrobozCo malware," "FrobozCo spyware," "FrobozCo adware," "WidgetWare malware," "Widget-Ware spyware," and "WidgetWare adware."

- Make sure your computer is behind the right kind of device so that bad guys can't easily take advantage of the problems in it. You can actually do this from your computer on Windows:

  1. Access the Start menu, then select All Programs → Accessories → Command Prompt.

  2. In the window that appears, type `ipconfig` and press Enter.

  3. If you are connected via wireless, look for the Ethernet Adaptor Wireless Network Connection section. If you are connected by a physical wire, look for the Ethernet Adaptor Local Area Connection section. In the appropriate section, look at the line that starts "IP Address". If the number on that line starts with 10, 192.168, or 172, where 172 is followed by any number from 16 to 31, you are fine.

  4. If you're not fine, you really need a geek in your life. Tell her you need to be behind NAT.

- Try to make sure you only connect to wireless systems that require passwords. Do not stay connected if a wireless network switches from requiring a password to not requiring one. Also, try to avoid public wireless access points.

Here are the safety rules I give my children (the explanations are very necessary, I've found):

- Don't give your passwords to anybody except your parents, not even your real-life friends.

- Don't download or install any programs without my permission. Bad stuff often gets packaged with good stuff. If it's safe, I will let you download it.

- Don't click on any ads without my permission, even if it looks like fun or like you're going to get something for free.

- Don't open email attachments without my permission. If it's from someone you don't know, there's a very good chance it's bad, and if it's from someone you do know, it could still be a virus.

- Don't give any personal information about yourself to people that you don't actually know in real life (particularly, last name, address, or phone number) without my permission.

- Lots of ads try not to look like ads to trick you into clicking. If you see that "someone has a crush on you!", don't click on it.

- Only go to green websites (this assumes you have SiteAdvisor installed). If you somehow find yourself on a red site, close the window immediately.

- If you have any doubt whatsoever, ask me.

CHAPTER 18

Snake Oil: Legitimate Vendors Sell It, Too

Traditionally, when security experts talk about snake oil products (i.e., security products that don't actually offer any security), they are usually only brave enough to call out products from dubious companies that make claims that are obviously false—almost always around cryptography. Few people call out venture-backed companies with well-known people on the management team.

This is partially because with most products, it's not so clear-cut whether they are crapware. That is, the company's marketing department can always find someone happy with the product, so it turns into a battle of credibility and opinion. The technical merits become secondary. A more common issue is that products do something to help, but they're not as awesome as their vendors would have you believe.

At the end of the day, if we say snake oil products are ones that don't do what the marketing leads customers to believe they do, many reputable security companies peddle snake oil.

For example, consider the company Trusteer. It's backed by the firm U.S. Venture Partners. It has some seasoned veterans on its team, and some smart people. Plus, it has one big customer, ING Direct, who I'll assume is happy with them.

Trusteer's product is snake oil.

Its marketing claims that its product, Rapport, "...protects login credentials and transactions, from desktop to Website, even if a computer is infected with malware." When I first heard this claim, I heard it directly from the company president's mouth when he was explaining to me what the company does (incidentally, I thought he was a good guy who genuinely believed in the marketing). I asked, "Is this even going to work when malware writers start targeting your software?" He said, "Yes," and that the company's technique will protect your personal info, no matter what infection is on your machine.

While there are a few ways you could make claims like that and have it be defensible, the solution he explained to me didn't sound like it would do that job. Basically, Trusteer puts its code on your machine, and that code obfuscates stuff. A determined attacker should eventually be able to figure out what that code is doing and undo it or disable it.

The only way I can imagine Trusteer defending its technical claims is for it to say, "Well, we sit in the kernel, and malware can't touch us if it's running with regular user privileges." But in reality, there is plenty of malware that gets inside the kernel. Often, the bad guy just tricks the user into installing something with administrative privileges.

A few days ago, a friend sent me a link with a video that shows *custom malware that has no problem defeating Trusteer's protection*.[1] The product does not do what the company claims.

If I were part of Trusteer, I'd counter this claim of snake oil by saying, "Well, we never expected people to think it works all the time, just that it works most of the time." I wonder if ING Direct knew that when it started offering its product. Because now, ING Direct is going to its banking customers with a product that makes people feel like they don't have to worry about whether they're infected anymore. Why pay for AV when the only thing you're worried about is identity theft?

Even if Trusteer's marketing claims reflected the reality of its technology, I think it promotes a false sense of security. In short, trusting this product to do the job it claims to do only puts you at risk,

---

[1] *http://epifail.narod.ru/rapport.html*

particularly because it's not a huge stretch to think that if you're going to get infected, it could easily be by something that can disable Trusteer's product. In fact, if enough people are using Trusteer's product, that kind of malware would certainly get pretty common.

But I suppose that if you do understand the risks, this product is better than nothing. Certainly, if you think you have a good chance of being infected, you shouldn't do online banking at all, you should worry about the infection. But if you don't think you are, then this product could actually help some of the time, when it turns out you actually were infected.

As you can see, the line between snake oil and a legitimate product is often all in the marketing. As a general rule of thumb, security companies want to make you think you're as secure as possible. Many of them are happy to lead you to believe that you're more secure than you actually are, which could end up putting you in a bad situation.

Therefore, it's generally worth doing your homework on security products you buy, to make sure you have at least a high-level understanding of the technical merits and the drawbacks.

CHAPTER 19

Living in Fear?

I am a bit ashamed to admit that I watch the TV show *24*. While I enjoy the bubblegum plot and the action, what I really like most about it is something else entirely.

24 is a show about homeland security. It paints a picture of a world where we just barely survive all kinds of terrorist activities, more by luck than anything else. It portrays a world where Homeland Security is not effective whatsoever, mainly because good people are choked by bureaucracy, and only people who are willing to bend the rules will get good results.

In the world of *24*, they talk a lot about computer security. Bad guys hack government machines. Good guys hack government machines. What I love, though, is to laugh at their absurd security and technology discussions.

For instance, in the world of *24*, the entire government is protected by one big firewall. When the bad guys control the firewall, they're instantly capable of doing anything they want on any computer in the U.S. government. In one recent episode, the bad guys used their access to take over the FAA flight systems.

There's a lot wrong with that scenario. First, if you can bypass a firewall, it doesn't automatically give you full access to the machines behind it—it just allows you to see those machines in the first place. You still have to find a way onto the machines.

And then, does anyone really expect the FAA to connect the air traffic control systems to systems that can access the public Internet? Sure, there may be some way onto that network because of people doing things that are against policy, meaning it's probably *possible* to hack the FAA from the Internet at large, but it would be extraordinarily difficult to leverage such a mistake. How do bad guys know which computers have access to the FAA? Are they going to break in to every machine they can in the U.S. and try to check? Bad guys would be a lot better off strong-arming an FAA employee to let them use a system. And even then, I will bet there are systems in place to help prevent misuse, even from legitimate users.

Now, good guys do indeed try to break in to bad guys' machines. I know people who do work on behalf of the U.S. government, finding security problems in software that the government can strategically exploit (hopefully, they don't use this kind of stuff on their own citizens). But doing things on the scale shown on a show like 24 is extremely difficult, especially without people on the inside.

Another example that I love is when they take a crappy photo or video (say, for instance, from a surveillance camera) and then "enhance" things to get all sorts of detail. While it's possible to make minor enhancements to pictures, the way it is portrayed on 24 could only be real if magic were real.

I think 24 is pandering to post-9/11 fears, attempting to give people the impression that the world is a far less safe place than it actually is. Are terrorists going to try to blow up all of the nuclear power plants in the U.S., like they did a few seasons ago on 24? Probably not—that's unrealistic for a terrorist group of any size. For a small group, there would need to be a single point of failure. On the show, there was some magic device that gave access to all nuclear power plant generators. That's pure fantasy!

The problem with a big terrorist group trying to launch a large coordinated attack is that the more people involved, the more risk there is of someone identifying key players in the terrorist network and shutting it down (even if the individual bad guys don't know about their targets until the last minute, as was the case with 9/11). Blowing up even 20 power plants is overambitious and likely to fail.

If I were a terrorist,[1] I'd be happy with blowing up one or two, and telling the world we could, at more or less any time, do the same to dozens of other plants. That is, the terrorists would be at their most effective if their attacks work and spread fear.

Even in 9/11, the bad guys only tried to take a handful of planes and ram them into a small number of monuments. That was enough to inspire mass fear. If they had gone after 40 planes, they would have had all sorts of complications, including difficulties finding enough trained pilots in the U.S. who were willing to go on suicide missions for that cause.

If the terrorists were really in a good position to run a guerrilla war on our turf, they wouldn't go to the effort to hit high-value targets on a very infrequent basis. It's just too much work!

Instead, the terrorists would make lives miserable with a bit of guerrilla warfare, with all the bad guys acting on their own or in independent small groups. They would blow up lots of bridges on interstates to make it difficult for people to get where they want to go. They would blow up train tracks to derail trains. They would detonate bombs in low-security areas of cities with lots of people (e.g., Times Square during a summer day). This kind of a war would cause lots of fear, particularly in urban areas. And it would cause our society to spend lots of money, both in undoing the damage and in adding security measures to prevent future attacks.

But the bad guys don't do these kinds of things. I believe there just aren't enough people like that who have made it to America. It's pretty tough to get a visa if you're from a country with vastly different ideologies from ours. The overwhelming majority of the people who do get visas have jobs or family waiting for them. Those people are usually more interested in their own lives than giving it all up for politics, especially when they interact with people and learn that while our cultures are different, there are plenty of good people here (just like in every other part of the world). Sure, border security will never be perfect, and there always will be a few people who get through, but it would be tough for true malcontents to build a big enough anti-American

---

[1] My copyeditor said I would "make a great terrorist!!" I guess that means I'm making her job too difficult!

population to really cause consistent chaos for a long time. So, it just doesn't happen.

The world is becoming a safer and safer place, all things considered. Violent crime rates have been dropping for a long time now. We do have more security measures, yet we are far more worried about security issues. We don't let kids out of our sight until they're 16. For instance, when I was 8, I used to ride my bike all around the town I grew up in, without any parental supervision (just be home by supper!). Today, that's child endangerment. Heck, I've seen a group of parents yelling at another parent for leaving an 8-year-old kid to wait by himself outside a restaurant in an amusement park, while the parent was inside using the bathroom.

I think this culture of paranoia has developed because we are bombarded by bad stuff. It dominates the news and shows like *24*. Even if people tell us the statistics and we know we're safer, we don't feel safer, because of that overexposure through TV, magazines, the Internet, and so on.

In my argument so far, I've basically implied that national security is largely ineffective. I think that's a true statement, but it's not a full picture. Yes, it's ineffective, because bad guys will always have easy targets, like bridges and crowds, but there are a couple of important questions related to this:

- Are we better off because of the security we do have?
- Would it be worth the cost to have better security?
- Could we better spend our existing dollars on security to get us better protection?

For the first question, a lot of people would argue that most of our security is just "theater." Consider airline security—it looks impressive, but it clearly doesn't work as well as it should. Multiple times I've seen news stories about people successfully sneaking loaded guns through security checkpoints (usually to test how effective the security screeners are). Bad guys will often forgo the checkpoint completely, and just leverage delivery people or other workers with access to the tarmac.

I personally think that this perspective is a bit too cynical. No, airport security does not work too well. However, it can detect some kinds of things with good enough odds that bad guys would probably not want to risk trying to walk through a checkpoint with loaded pistols in their bags. Even though there are many holes, the system we do have makes the bad guys work a lot harder and spend a lot more in order to reduce their risks and increase their odds of getting through.

In the extreme example, if we got rid of air travel security altogether, it would be pretty easy for terrorists to go on suicide missions or hijackings. It seems likely that the number of incidents would go up. Remember the days when hijackings were pretty common occurrences? I remember it happening a lot when I was a kid. Funny, those flights tended not to originate in the U.S. where there was security screening, but in countries with no screening. Now basic screening is universal.

Some people might agree with me but still ask why we have to take off our shoes, unpack our laptops, and check most of our liquids. That kind of screening doesn't seem to be cost-effective. It isn't clear how big the real threat would be, but it's probably pretty small. Yet, it greatly inconveniences everybody.

I think that's probably true. Some security experts call this kind of stuff "security theater." The TSA puts on a great show at the checkpoints, but you're really not appreciably more secure when flying than you were before 9/11.

But there's some hidden value here—it makes people *feel* safer. Whether it works well or poorly, it is better than nothing and it makes people feel better.

As for the question of whether the U.S. could be spending money on homeland security more effectively, that's a much more difficult question to answer. In theory, there should be tons of ways to make cost-effective improvements. In practice, government bureaucracy and the realities of running a large organization make it extremely difficult.

CHAPTER 20

Is Apple Really More Secure?

This is a pretty fun topic because people get so emotional about it, on both sides.

Before I register my opinion, I need to be clear that I've been operating almost exclusively on a Mac since OS X came out in early 2001. I grew up in Unix, and never liked the lack of usability in Windows, so it was a good fit. However, I don't have any particular interest in making Apple look better than it really is, particularly when it comes to security. So, I don't really consider myself a "fan boy," but I do know plenty of people over in Apple, and I have some insight into what its product security team looks like.

Apple and its fan boys will talk about how its platform is more secure because there is so little malware for it.

Security people will talk about how there are plenty of vulnerabilities published for OS X, and that it is certainly not inherently more secure than other operating systems.

Both sides are correct! Yes, there are plenty of vulnerabilities in OS X. I wouldn't necessarily say it's an undue number—we all know secure software is difficult to write, and there are going to be problems. And in anything as large as an operating system, there are always going to be more security holes to find. I think what's important is that Apple seems to take things seriously and get patches out in a timely manner when things go public (disclosure tends to be when the malware starts coming out).

At the same time, it's true that, from what I've seen, there are only about half a dozen truly unique pieces of malware out there (including the Leap Worm, the RSPlug Trojan, and the OSX_ LAMZEV backdoor). No matter how many vulnerabilities there have been in the OS, almost none of them has been leveraged by real malware. It's clear that it's far less risky (at the moment) to be an OS X user than a Windows user, even though OS X users probably aren't running AV, and even though Microsoft has spent billions improving the security of its offerings.

What gives??!! Why don't bad guys seem to be too interested in OS X? This is the really interesting question. It seems like OS X should be a huge target, since the market share is now so high— apparently, over 20% of new machines sold in the U.S. are Macs (though Gartner claims its market share is 6%). No matter who is right on the market share issue, I'll hazard a guess and say that about 7–10% of computers actually in use at any given moment are Apples (at least in the U.S.). Even if it's only 3%, that seems like a huge base of PCs that should be an appealing target to bad guys looking to build a legion of infected hosts to use in spam campaigns, ad delivery, and so on—particularly considering that most people running Macs don't run AV (and that includes me!).

If you look at reported sales figures, Apple sold about 6 million laptops and 4 million desktops in 2007. Also, I'd venture to guess that most Mac owners are like me—they have a laptop as their primary machine, but they still have a desktop or two sitting around, maybe to have the bigger drive for all their photos, music, and movies, or as a dedicated media editing workstation. But they don't really install a lot of software from the Internet on those machines or spend too much time browsing the Web. I've got two Apple desktops that are almost exclusively media PCs (when kids are around, they occasionally end up browsing to sites like Disney.com or webkinz.com while supervised). And I've got a couple that are test machines and are usually turned off.

Those desktops typically aren't doing anything too risky, because they are secondary machines for most people. It's the laptops that we use to surf the shady side of the Internet. The laptops are the bulk of the Macs that get day-to-day Internet use (I'd guess north of 80%).

If I were a bad guy, I'd be far less interested in "owning" a machine that changes location a lot and is frequently closed. It's a lot harder to count on those resources, contact them, and leverage them. Since there are so few desktops in use, I'd posit that Apple has a much smaller market share in terms of machines that are useful to attackers.

Plus, it costs more to produce malware for OS X because the tools that lower the cost aren't available. I have not yet seen anything for OS X akin to the Pinch malware creation tool. Therefore, if you're a bad guy, you need to come up with Apple development skills, whereas before, you didn't need to have any particular skills at all.

Eventually, Apples might be the lowest-hanging fruit, but there seem to be plenty of Windows PCs that are still ready to be owned. And for most people, it is far less costly to own those PCs. Therefore, simple malware economics is doing a good job of protecting Mac users—no AV necessary.

I'm sure it will eventually become more cost-effective for bad guys to target Macs, and it may end up getting harder for bad guys to find Windows PCs that aren't already owned. When that day comes and there are real threats out there for OS X, that's when it will be important to have some malware protection on your Mac. Until then, that's one less thing I have to buy!

CHAPTER 21

OK, Your Mobile Phone Is Insecure; Should You Care?

Security vendors have long been predicting that bad guys are soon going to be targeting mobile phones. There's a "boy who cried wolf" effect here. People have heard the prediction so many times that they have stopped listening.

As far as I can tell, this prediction first emerged in 2000. AV vendors have had mobile phone products out there since 2003, maybe earlier (Airscanner seems to be the oldest mobile phone security product I can find, and it was clearly out no later than 2003). Every year brings new predictions and new products. Yet, there is almost no true malware for mobile phones. There really is no good reason to be listening to the doom and gloom.

The big question here is why the bad guys haven't gone after mobile platforms. After all, there were almost as many smartphones sold last year as there were laptop computers (both in the 120–125 million range).

And, despite what some people believe, there is money to be made from hacking phones. A bad guy could still use malware on a phone to do things like send spam. But there are other things a bad guy can do. For example, in Europe, there's a widely adopted technology called *pay-by-SMS*, where you can pay for things just by sending a text message. You can pay for online things this way, but you can also buy sodas from soda machines, and things like that. A bad guy could break in to a phone in Germany and use it to buy himself a soda in Finland using pay-by-SMS technology.

There has been real malware for the Symbian smartphone operating system (currently the most popular smartphone OS, found on many Nokia and Sony Ericsson phones) that can do that kind of thing.

Still, there's no mobile malware epidemic, only a few dozen pieces of bad software. What gives?

Well, there are lots of little things that make life difficult for the bad guy:

- Mobile providers have pretty good network security for their phones. Bad guys can't find a particular phone by network address—the phone has to be actively communicating with them. And many smartphones (for example, the iPhone) make it tough for applications to stay in constant communication. If a bad guy has a botnet with lots of mobile phones, she may have a hard time addressing a lot of her bots in a timely manner. But then again, if there's enough scale, it's not clear whether this is a big deal. Plus, even the iPhone is being dragged kicking and screaming into supporting *push* technology, where applications don't have to be actively running to receive messages from the servers they deal with frequently.

- Mobile phones traditionally haven't had awesome processing power, which means that if malware is running, people are highly likely to notice that their user experience sucks. These days, malware is all about trying to be stealthy! Of course, mobile processing power keeps getting more and more powerful, and already this isn't too much of a concern on the newest platforms.

- On most mobile phone platforms, it is very challenging to install and run a mobile application without the user noticing that something fishy is happening. On the iPhone, for instance, there's no real way to install apps that don't come from the iPhone store, unless there is a wider security problem on the phone (a flaw in the underlying software). So bad guys either need to find these flaws or build their apps so that end users are happy to install them.

- Because of phone providers' network security, it's almost impossible to install malware on the phone without the user taking some action. Not only does a bad guy need to social-engineer people, but most smartphone users don't actually use the Internet too much (in the U.S., a lot of them don't even know how to use text messaging).

- Having a foothold on one phone doesn't significantly improve a bad guy's ability to attack other phones. It's not like corporate worlds where a bad guy can break in to one machine, then snoop passwords on the same subnet and scan for vulnerable services on other machines behind the corporate firewall.

- Mobile phone operating systems often make it very difficult to mess with another application. For instance, if a bad guy can get a user to install a bad program, it may still be impossible to see the passwords typed into the mobile web browser.

When you look at all of these factors, it's clear that it's generally tough to get malware onto a mobile phone and have it run. This is partially because there are so few users, partially because of usability issues, and partially because of technical challenges.

Sure, there will always be the occasional virus for smartphones, but I don't see an epidemic emerging. At the end of the day, there is still lower-hanging fruit for the bad guys. It is still far easier for them to make money attacking traditional PCs and laptops then going after mobile phones. That may eventually change, but I'm not going to hold my breath.

CHAPTER 22

Do AV Vendors Write Their Own Viruses?

One frequent (and typically serious) question I get is whether McAfee has people writing and spreading viruses to increase the need for its own product.

I've seen other people I know who work for a big AV company get asked that question, and the answer is often an indignant, "Of course not," primarily because that would be illegal. In most people's minds, that's defensive, and might be taken as guilt.

Personally, I think I'm ethical, and if McAfee were doing something that explicitly illegal, I'd very much feel the obligation to blow the whistle. Certainly, I wouldn't have gone back to the company for a second tour of duty.

The short answer is, of course, no; at least at McAfee (and hopefully everywhere else), that does not happen. But a more accurate answer would be that even though the business doesn't condone it, there might be some very slim chance that somewhere somebody in the organization is a maverick producing malware.

If that were to happen, it seems highly unlikely that the incentive would be to improve company performance. It's such an indirect way to benefit the company for a smart engineer who is good enough to write malware, and he or she would know it's unethical. If the employee were that unethical, I suspect he'd be more inclined to do it to benefit himself, and the fact that he was at a big company would be incidental.

I'm sure that this kind of thing has happened in the lifetime of our industry, but as far as I'm aware, there's never been a major AV player that would condone that kind of thing (though I have heard rumors that some of the small companies have done it to give themselves the publicity of doing better than the big guys. I generally don't find these rumors too credible).

In fact, McAfee went quite far in its attempts to ensure that no malware accidentally spread from within the company if it could be avoided. All malware samples were supposed to be analyzed in air-gapped labs (meaning no network connection to the outside world and tight control over what people can bring in and out). If samples were not in an air-gapped lab, they weren't supposed to be in a format in which they might be able to execute. Generally, this meant storing them in password-protected ZIP files. Even though the password was always the same and well known, this practice kept people from accidentally running infected files.

No, there was never any need for any security vendor to build its own malware. It's clearly quite profitable for other people to write malware (it's tough to even hazard a guess at the market size, but most educated estimates do seem to agree on it being a multibillion-dollar business). Plus, it is incredibly easy to create sophisticated malware that can disable AV products and capture passwords. It's so simple, you don't need to know how to program. Anyone who wants to write malware badly enough can do it. The trick is all in spreading the resulting software—making it likely that other people will get it installed without having it trace back to you.

The barrier to entry is basically zero, particularly for a competent social engineer. Malware is going to go where the money is, particularly since the levels of risk are so low. There are plenty of countries where you can perform nefarious deeds without worrying too much about the government coming after you. You can launch malware campaigns or spam campaigns from the safety of public Internet terminals.

CHAPTER 23

One Simple Fix for the AV Industry

What if I told you that the AV industry as a whole could reduce its operating costs on malware research, while providing customers with vastly better protection? Sounds like a pipe dream, but I say it isn't: all the AV industry has to do is organize itself to solve "the packer problem."

First, let me say that I think most of the AV industry is headed into the hurt locker. Today, research labs get thousands of unique malware samples a day (about two to six thousand, if you look at unique executables). And while a lot of the samples can be detected automatically, a lot of them can't. Most vendors can't keep up, even the ones with dozens of people doing AV research. Detection rates are way down and operational costs have to go up in order to keep up, at least while we wait for AV technology to improve.

Let's get to the packer problem, which is probably the single biggest problem in the AV space. The bad guys use *packing* software and encryption software to obfuscate their malware. I'll give you a high-level overview of the problem (which is responsible for most accuracy problems in AV software), and then I'll talk about the impact and what the AV industry should be doing about it.

Packing software basically encodes a binary, supposedly to make it smaller. The result is a binary that unpacks itself before the original binary runs. The packed binary will mostly look like gibberish.

An AV vendor that's just looking at a static version of the software can tell that there's some sort of encoding on the binary, but it may have big problems getting more information than that.

It might be possible to tell what's going on by looking at the unpack routine in the executable, and then the vendor can unpack it and analyze the binary (it might be packed multiple times, of course). Once the AV vendor can analyze the binary, its job is generally much, much easier.

The game here is for the bad guys to make it as challenging as possible for the good guys to unpack (or unencrypt) their malware. It's much easier for the bad guy to use one basic piece of malware and keep repackaging it over and over again. That way, if a vendor identifies one particular executable as bad, it probably isn't going to catch a repacked version of that executable. Bad guys are getting really sophisticated, changing the packing for a piece of software regularly (say, every hour, every 100 downloads, or even on the fly).

This is the point where a lot of techies say, "That's absurd! Surely, legitimate vendors don't need to do the same kinds of things. The AV vendors should be able to just see if something looks packed and deny it!" Unfortunately, the world is more complicated than that. Many legitimate software vendors like to keep their competitors from prying out their trade secrets, so they will use the same tools and techniques to obfuscate their code (let's be realistic, saving disk space for the stored binary is not much of a concern—in practice, the in-memory size is much more important to resource constraints).

The good guys are going to want to use the same tools the bad guys are, because they both really want to do everything possible to keep people out. So even when one can differentiate the tool that was used, the AV vendor can't just categorically block everything produced with that tool. The vendor also needs to go ahead and unpack the software and see if it is actually bad. That sucks because it is pretty easy for the bad guys to create a new packer/ encryptor that will thwart existing automated attempts to unpack/ decrypt. And on the flip side, it's basically impossible to write something generic that unpacks/decrypts.

One approach that AV vendors use is to try to take packed samples and see what they do. There are a number of variations on this approach. Here are some degrees of freedom:

- They can run malware samples for real (on real hardware or on a virtual machine), or they can run them on a custom emulator.
- They can try to determine when the sample is fully unpacked and then analyze the static image in memory. Or they can just forget about that and try to watch for signs of bad behavior.
- They can try to do all this in the company's backend or they can do it on their customer's PCs.

Most companies mix and match, deploying several combinations of the aforementioned ideas. For instance, the desktop AV product may contain an emulation engine that tries to unpack things and then analyze the results. Companies may also have backend virtual systems that process malware samples to analyze their behaviors.

That all sounds well and good, but it turns out that these systems don't have the success rate one might like. For instance, if an AV company is running an emulator on the end user's machine, what's to stop a bad guy from reverse-engineering it, or at least testing against it, until the malware no longer triggers anything? Generally, that's a good way to avoid detection, at least until a future content update. And there are lots of tricks a bad guy could use to prevent backend analysis from triggering; simple stuff like, "don't show malware behaviors if running on a virtual machine" or, "don't misbehave except in this 10-minute window on the first Friday of the month," tends to work pretty well, depending on the system.

As a result, there's an ongoing arms race here, and the bad guys are in a much stronger position.

The AV industry can collectively solve its problem if the companies all stand together. I propose they start a Consortium for Interoperability with Security Technology (it's a CIST, not a tumor). Put a date in the sand. Perhaps after 2010, all packed/encrypted software, as well as abnormally self-modifying software, will be flagged automatically as malware, unless one of the following is true:

- The application is signed by a vendor and signing credentials are registered with CIST.
- The application was independently registered with CIST.

Most applications won't need a digital signature or any sort of registering, because they won't be encrypted or packed. Companies that feel the need to protect their IPs will be willing to dish out the pittance for code signing credentials and registration of those credentials. Additionally, registered companies should be able to, one time only, provide CIST with a set of legacy applications that they'd like to ensure are not accidentally flagged as malware.

There certainly are some minor technical issues here, such as whether all code needs to be signed, how one specifies what is being signed, and so on. I'd personally want to see one manifest per executable enumerating the shared libraries it uses, and a signature over all those elements. But these are minor issues that can certainly be addressed.

Of course, CIST needs to be able to revoke people's certificates if it finds people who are actually peddling malware. If registration is done properly, this system would introduce some real accountability, so when someone did try to game the system, it would be easier to hunt him down and kick the crap out of him.

The AV industry needs to do this for its own sake. There needs to be a central registry for packed/encrypted applications, for the good of all mankind. This problem is not only expensive; it is starting to hurt reputations of AV vendors due to bad detection. Wouldn't it be nice if we could go back to the days when we only saw a few truly unique pieces of malware a day (things not easily identifiable as slight variants of other pieces of malware)? If we could remove the packer problem, that's more or less where we would be.

CHAPTER 24

Open Source Security: A Red Herring

If you're reading this book, there's a good chance you're at least familiar with the open source software movement. Lots of people, from students to professionals working part-time, write free software that anybody else can take and modify, if they so desire. A surprising number of large companies make major contributions to open source software, including giant IBM. Many important pieces of software are open source, including Apache, which is the number-one web server platform (about half the websites on the Internet use Apache).

About a decade ago, a guy named Eric S. Raymond started evangelizing open source outside the world of the super geeks, into the corporate world, governments, and so on. One of the claims he made was that open source software was more secure than closed source software because of the "many eyeballs" theory. He believed that, because the source is freely available, lots of people will look for security flaws in it in a way that isn't going to happen in the commercial world.

That argument is BS, and I have said so pretty loudly throughout the past decade.

Don't get me wrong—I love open source software! But, typically, when I write an article on this topic, people will say something like, "Clearly you don't know anything about open source, because if you did, you would realize it is just so much better than commercial software!" Then I mention that I've written a lot of open source software, including Mailman, the leading mailing list manager, which has maintained its popularity over the last 12 years.

The case for open source being more secure isn't too well defined. The "many eyeballs" effect was the cornerstone of the original argument.

But lots of things in the security world aren't well defined. What does it mean for one program to be more secure than another? You could have two programs, A and B. Program A could have 1,000 security vulnerabilities and program B could have only 1. If the bad guys never find the 1,000 in program A, but they do find the one in program B, which is more secure? I think that's all a matter of definition. To my mind, program A has more security vulnerabilities, and program B puts users more at risk.

The issue of open source security, then, actually consists of two different questions:

- Do open source programs tend to have more or fewer vulnerabilities than closed source programs? The question here is really about the bug rate, because there is clearly a lot more commercial software out there.

- Are open source users more or less likely to suffer from a security problem?

I'll try to address both of these, but I think the second is far more important. For instance, I once owned a software service that, when I inherited it, required over 200 servers to handle the load, because the code was all written in Java. Now, even though the user base is larger (because it was rewritten for performance in the C programming language), the entire system runs quite comfortably on eight machines (and could run on far fewer). The new system costs a *lot* less to operate. The total cost savings for all the machines that I don't have to run dwarfs the expected additional cost of dealing with security vulnerabilities. In fact, because the system is closed and only runs within a single company (it is software as a service, not something that goes on an end user's desktop), and because we did invest in secure development practices, the future cost of dealing with vulnerabilities might even be zero, even if there are big security vulnerabilities waiting to be found.

Let's look at some of the major factors that contribute to both of our questions about how secure programs will be:

The security knowledge of the people who design and write the code
The more you understand about security problems, the more likely you are to avoid the kinds of problems you know about. This impacts both open source and proprietary software. There are high school kids working on prominent open source projects who are uneducated about security issues, but then again, most open source people are passionate about programming and know something about security (or at least, think they know something). In the commercial world, there are a lot of developers who don't enjoy their jobs; they only enjoy cashing the paycheck. On the other hand, many open source developers, being self-trained, actually don't have a well-rounded education of software security. They know about a few things, but there's a lot they typically haven't been exposed to. However, most medium and large development organizations offer training for their development teams to teach them about security issues.

I have seen some evidence from people measuring the effectiveness of training that suggests that software security training doesn't work very well. It seems that, even for highly rated teachers, most developers forget much of what they learn within six months of the training. Based on everything I've seen, I believe that passionate people are going to retain training better. However, I think that it is important to be passionate about security. Even in the open source world, people who are passionate about their individual products couldn't care less about security, and won't really learn.

The level of performance from the people building code
By this, I mean that even people who understand security problems are not immune to them. As a developer, if you're focused on a feature you're having problems with, it may be very easy to let a security issue slip by. I think that commercial development environments often encourage better discipline here. In my experience, commercial environments are vastly more likely to schedule in explicit time for developers to do security tasks, or to put tools in place to enforce good coding practices. For instance, many commercial organizations have tools that prevent individuals from adding code that match some definition of "risky." That's a very uncommon practice in the open source world.

The technology choices the development team makes

For instance, some people will write in the C programming language because they need its performance for their applications. Commercial environments are far more likely to pay to use tools that help produce more secure software; even though there are some free tools that everyone can use, commercial companies are a whole lot more willing, on average, to spend money on the problem. And, because there is money to be spent, the commercial tools are usually a lot more useful than the free tools.

The ease with which people could find security problems

If the person looking for security vulnerabilities has the source code and the ability to run the program, that's a best-case scenario. If you take away the source code, the job generally gets much harder. Yes, there are often issues that can be found pretty easily without looking at the source code (through fuzz testing, for example), but anyone can do those things. And once all the low-hanging fruit is gone, you've got to start looking at the actual code of the program. The source code shows a high-level, easy-to-understand representation of the code that the computer actually runs. If you don't have that, you have to look at something far more low-level. It's still possible, but far fewer people have the skill set (reverse-engineering), and even for the people who do, the level of effort increases tremendously.

Even if you're more of a target because you're creating commercial software, increasing the cost of finding bugs means that the people looking for them will generally have to choose either to spend more or find fewer bugs. Since the skill set is so technical and there isn't a big supply of people possessing it, it's obvious that researchers are finding far fewer bugs than they would if they had the source code.

Plus, in a Software-as-a-Service model, the world at large doesn't even get the benefit of having a program to reverse-engineer.

The actions that people take when they find bugs

There are plenty of security researchers finding security bugs and publishing them to the world. That puts people at risk.

Then there are a few people looking for security bugs in order to use them for their own nefarious purposes. When a company does its own auditing or pays for someone else to do auditing, it generally isn't going to tell the world about the problems—it's just going to fix them silently. If nobody else knows about the problem, people are generally safer, especially since they don't typically upgrade very often, even if there are security issues.

How quickly users upgrade

If users upgrade quickly, they'll be less at risk, assuming software gets safer with each new release. Sometimes that's not true, because new code can add new bugs. If bad guys find out about bugs in a new version, the old version might still be safe. Generally, it is probably smart to always upgrade quickly, if all you care about is risk reduction (there may be other reasons not to upgrade, like cost, more bugs in the new version, and so on).

The number and skills of the people looking for security problems

Most people who have access to open source code don't look at it, or don't put in the effort required to understand much of it, if they do give it a casual look. Most of the people who really dig in do so only to fix a bug or add a feature they wanted. There is a community of people who are trying to find bugs in programs, but they are generally trying to boost their reputations (some do look for flaws in order to use them maliciously). But the bad guys mainly just use the flaws that security researchers find (the security researchers hope they are actually making software more safe by helping get rid of the problems). Security researchers might use their time to look at the top pieces of open source, but then again, if the "many eyeballs" theory is correct, most of the things have been picked over pretty well (and are probably pretty secure). But for the many open source programs that have some users but wouldn't be prestigious (meaning they're not important enough to be resume-building for a vulnerability finder), are they going to get the eyeballs looking for security problems? Or are the good security auditors going to take their skills to high-profile commercial targets? There are tons more prominent programs from closed vendors than there are from open source vendors, and large software companies tend to have hundreds of products. If you can find a product from a major vendor that doesn't have a big budget (because it doesn't have many users), that might be a great place to go looking for security bugs, because there's a good chance the security practices won't be up to par for the rest of the company. And, unlike in the open source world, it doesn't matter that there aren't many users; you will get credit from your peers because you found a problem in software from a major vendor.

Yes, it can be a whole lot tougher to find bugs when you don't have the source code, but it's not impossible. Sometimes it's downright easy, if you build the right kind of simple testing tools. In fact, doing the harder work makes you more awesome in the eyes of your peers. Plus, there may actually be more bugs waiting to be found in commercial software. Since commercial software projects tend to be a lot bigger than open source projects, even if a commercial program is likely to have a lower defect rate than an open source project (not a given, of course), there may very well be far more security bugs in the program, because there are far more lines of code.

At the end of the day, I'd say there are probably only a couple thousand full-time equivalents looking for security problems in software. The important stuff in the open source world is picked over pretty well, but the average large corporation probably hasn't gotten too much attention, particularly because the workload is likely to be higher to find bugs.

Plus, companies are more willing to spend money on finding security problems, either directly by hiring people to take a look, or indirectly by having staff spend time on the problem (though companies will often spend money for tools to help in the process). A big driver here is the U.S. government, which is generally afraid of open source (though, thankfully, that is slowly changing). However, I have seen the government require commercial vendors to get an external security audit before it will buy. I have even seen it invest in doing the audit itself.

All in all, I don't think it necessarily follows that open source is getting more eyeballs. Probably the top programs are, but when you look at the average commercial product from a major vendor, I think there's a good chance that it has received more attention.

For the most part, I think the issue of whether source is open or proprietary is a red herring. Pure software-as-a-service/web-based delivery is an exception. I think there is clearly an advantage to keeping the source closed in that case.

Why a red herring? As geeks like to say, "Correlation is not causation." It's not really whether something is open or closed that leads to better software. A better indicator is how much money was spent on securing the software.

Here, the most popular software is generally best off. The most popular open source software gets reviewed more. The most popular commercial software typically has a large investment in training, tools, auditing, and so on.

Sure, there might be some pros to open source (maybe open source authors do tend to introduce fewer bugs, because there's a lot less code), and some advantages to closed source (the difficulty of finding the bugs that are there, for example).

However, there is no real evidence that any of these advantages of either model has a significant impact, whereas money and effort clearly do.

Getting a bit more specific, to answer the question, "Is open source or closed source more likely to yield more security bugs?", I would say, "There's no sure data, but whether or not the source is open is probably not a relevant factor if it's a popular product." There are, of course, relevant factors.

For example, money spent on avoiding bugs during design goes a *lot* further than money spent fixing a bad design. Email systems like Postfix and qmail probably have less of an investment in their security than Sendmail does, but all of Sendmail's investment came after it became clear that its design was poor and there were tons of bugs. On the other hand, the designers of Postfix and qmail were incredibly defensive when they were building the software.

Now, let's get back to the question, "Are users of the commercial version or the open source version more or less likely to be affected?"

Frankly, you're probably safest running all open source on a Linux box. But that's only because so few people use Linux machines that the bad guys don't invest their money here. If 80% of the world ran Linux, you'd probably be much safer running Windows! And if you ran all commercial software on the Linux box, except for the core OS itself, you'd probably be safer still.

In practice, most people want to run pretty mainstream environments, so this question only really matters when there's both open and closed alternatives that work on the same platform.

Here again, I see it boiling down to the popularity of the packages and other factors such as how the money was spent. And, of course, there's the matter of how many bugs there are in the program and how many of them have been found.

For instance, maybe Microsoft's Exchange server now has more security flaws left in it than Sendmail, but if bad guys find yet another new Sendmail bug, the Exchange users are going to be safer. Historically, you've been safer as an Exchange user (but safest as a qmail user).

All in all, you can argue the open versus closed issue forever, but there isn't strong evidence to suggest that that's the right question to be asking in the first place.

CHAPTER 25

Why SiteAdvisor Was Such a Good Idea

One of the first things I worked on at McAfee was the SiteAdvisor acquisition. For those who don't know, SiteAdvisor basically tells you which sites are good and which sites are bad. The end user sees a green check or a red "x" annotating web search results. If you browse to a web page, there's also an indicator of whether the site is good or bad.

The way SiteAdvisor does this is incredibly impressive. It basically tests the entire Web. It's tough to reach that kind of scale, but this tiny little startup did a great job of solving the major technical issues. Frankly, before seeing what the SiteAdvisor team did, I would have thought the approach was probably unworkable. It's no surprise at all that those guys were the first (by far) to come up with a credible product, because it was incredibly complex and seemed insane.

Plenty of people have had criticisms of the approach. For instance, before its acquisition by AVG, Exploit Prevention Labs (XPL) would criticize SiteAdvisor publicly for not doing real-time testing. SiteAdvisor does its testing offline and then periodically updates its master database, which clients then query. The theory was that it would catch more exploits because the result was based on right now, not when a third party tested. This was pretty self-serving of XPL, because it was peddling browser-based exploit detection that runs as you browse.

XPL's technology was fine, but even though it billed itself as competitive with SiteAdvisor, I considered XPL irrelevant because it did not provide much customer value. First, exploit detection is almost irrelevant to the web browsing experience. Well under half a percent of websites have an active exploit on it, and the sites that do are often not going to be found by browsing. The odds of someone browsing his way into an exploit are basically miniscule. This is particularly the case since most web traffic goes to a small number of sites, and those sites get enough traffic that they tend to have better security and are a lot less likely to be hosting some kind of exploit. While SiteAdvisor protects against this kind of thing, it wasn't a big threat to consumers in the first place.

SiteAdvisor's primary value is in telling people what else is wrong with a site. SiteAdvisor signs up for mailing lists and then looks to see if those mailing lists are going to spam you, and whether you will be able to unsubscribe from those lists. It tells you if you're going to be flooded with pop ups. It tells you whether a site you go to has downloads with spyware in it. These are things that are far more common on the Web and will actually have a big impact on people's daily browsing experiences.

For instance, right now, when I search for "screensavers" on Google, I can see that most links, including all the top ones, are likely to distribute adware. That's not something most people would think about without something like SiteAdvisor. And all this, despite the fact that Google has, for quite a long time, been trying to flag "bad" sites in its search results. Google also sticks to exploits instead of trying to make judgment calls about adware and so on.

With traditional host security solutions such as AV, the end consumer doesn't really get to see AV working, particularly when nothing bad is happening. Only people who download malware see anything working. Out of sight, out of mind! It's no surprise that consumers see less value than they used to in host security, and that their willingness to pay is plummeting. With SiteAdvisor, McAfee gets to show all its consumer users the company's value on a daily basis as they browse the Web, and does so in a nonintrusive way. That's the value I saw the second I walked through the door, and nobody I've seen has been able to come close to matching it in the three years since.

CHAPTER 26

Is There Anything We Can Do About Identity Theft?

One of the biggest drivers for IT security spending today is the threat of identity theft. The laws and regulations vary by region and by business, but many companies face liability if they are responsible for negligent data loss.

In reality, lots of data gets lost or stolen. According to the Privacy Rights Clearinghouse, in the United States alone, there have been over 215 million electronic data records lost since the beginning of 2005. Now, most of the time, those records aren't used in identity theft, because they are lost, not stolen. For example, McAfee once had an auditor leave a CD with employee data in a airplane seat pocket. The data almost certainly went out with the trash. But, it happens often enough that there is real risk to consumers.

Plus, there are traditional methods of stealing personal information that aren't counted, such as copying down credit card information at a restaurant, going through someone's garbage, and so on. The risk to the average consumer is high enough, particularly considering it can take weeks of phone calls to clear up the damage done, when it is possible at all. Some people are left with massive credit problems.

There are several ways to make small amounts of progress on the problem. For example, many companies have made significant investments in data encryption for laptops. That way, if an employee with personal data on his laptop actually loses the laptop, a potential thief won't be able to get data off of it.

Another technique that has a big practical impact for consumers is ensuring that the consumer's credit card never has to leave her sight in a transaction. In restaurants, instead of giving the waiter a credit card and having him disappear into the back, where he is free to copy everything down—including the verification number (CCV)—the waiter instead brings a portable card reader and allows you to swipe the card and watch the whole transaction at your table. This system is already widespread in many parts of the world, but the first major deployment of this technology in the U.S. only happened in 2007, with the Legal Seafood restaurant chain.

Still, these patchwork solutions don't eliminate enough risk, particularly in the U.S., where there is one huge point of failure—the Social Security number. Americans are compelled to use their Social Security numbers as a single identifier for most financial-related things. Basically, any time someone needs to run a credit check on you, he will require your Social Security number, and you will most likely give it to him. You have to give it to your credit card companies, mortgage brokers, and even the guy in your local cell phone store when he runs a credit check on you for your new phone.

If any one of the organizations to whom you gave the number loses it, or if someone steals your wallet with your Social Security card in it, then, with just a bit more personal information that is easy to get, a bad guy can open up a line of credit in your name that you probably wouldn't know about until it was too late.

Some people address this through credit monitoring services, but such services require a fairly expensive annual subscription, and even if the credit industry were to give them away for free (a very expensive proposition), there would be problems when people move, change their contact information, or are not financially sophisticated consumers.

Instead, it would be better if we could have identifiers that are as functional as the Social Security number but more secure, so that if someone steals it, she can't actually do anything to harm the victim's credit.

Technically, with modern cryptography, this is not too challenging a problem. Imagine a system in which you give each company that needs to track you financially a separate Social Security number that is still unique to you. The number could be computed by some piece of software running on your phone or a tiny smart card that you keep in your wallet. The number could be tied just to that vendor, too. For example, let's say that you apply for a loan at Fred's Bank. Fred's Bank would want an identifier for you that it could use for your credit check. It would give you its own identifier, which you would enter into your phone or whatever device generates your one-time identifiers. You could certainly specify what you wanted the vendor to be able to do with the identifier, such as allowing it only to run a single credit check, or, in the case of a mortgage company, you might allow multiple credit checks over a 30-day period.

With this kind of system in place, if you walked into a cell phone store and had a credit check run on you with this kind of identifier, employees of the store would not be able to take that identifier and use it to open up a checking account, because the bank would know that the number was not intended for them. If someone tried to check your credit with Equifax using a stolen number, Equifax would be able to see who you originally gave the number to, how long it was supposed to be valid, and what you were allowing that vendor to use it for. If some other organization tried to run a credit check with that number, Equifax would not allow it.

In this scenario, the one-time Social Security numbers could all start with a public prefix that is unique to you, much like your existing Social Security number. But the rest of the number would be specific to the use, and would be critical for a vendor to actually do anything with it.

Everything surrounding this scheme could be automated pretty easily with software. Let's say you were in a cellular store, which wanted to run a credit check. And let's say you had a little smartcard with the one-time Social Security number generator on it. You could stick the card in the store's reader, then enter a personal PIN to authorize generation of the one-time number (adding another layer of security, to protect against the card itself being stolen and used by another individual). Your card would then store a record of what it generated, which you could upload to your computer at home. The number would be uploaded automatically to the store, so nobody would have to bother writing it down (which is a good thing, because it would end up quite a bit longer than a traditional Social Security number). The whole scheme could also be implemented on a phone, using Bluetooth, or with a little reader using RFID.

Technologically, it would be no great challenge to design a highly secure scheme in line with what is described here. But just because it's technically feasible doesn't mean it would necessarily be able to happen. There are huge practical barriers for this scheme to be adopted.

The first big barrier is the standardization that would be necessary. The technical details need to be very precisely specified, because thousands of companies are going to need to implement parts of the system. Not all vendors will be building card readers, but many vendors will at least need to make modifications to their internal applications to handle the new numbers, which requires precise specification. The standardization process for an important piece of technology, even if it is a simple piece of technology, usually takes a minimum of three years, and can often take a lot longer than that. Plus, there will be many companies sitting at the standards table with conflicting agendas. For instance, the Bluetooth manufacturers might want to see the technology deployed through phones, whereas other vendors may prefer to see something cheaper based on smart cards. People will naturally tend to look for compromise solutions that will be all things to all vendors, even though they risk killing the technology by making it too confusing, difficult to use, or expensive.

And everything would have to be designed and implemented in a way that supports backward compatibility with existing Social Security numbers. This requires careful consideration to ensure that the cost of implementation and transition isn't higher than necessary.

Once a standard is far enough along that companies can feel comfortable starting to implement it, they need to actually do the work and test it, which can be time-consuming. Plus, the industry needs a financial incentive to support this new technique, which probably isn't going to be pushed from consumers. Instead, it's probably going to need to come from government regulation (which will take some time, though it could easily just refer to a standard).

The biggest challenge with a scheme like this is the cost, which is a large practical barrier to adoption. There are research and development costs to get new software and hardware developed, tested, and deployed. Then, individual vendors need to get and deploy their hardware and software, which will generally be a nontrivial task.

Then, software, and possibly smart card hardware, needs to make it into the hands of the end consumer. There's going to be a cost associated with the Social Security Administration validating people before giving them hardware, and then there is the actual cost of the hardware itself. How does that bill get covered? Undoubtedly, some subsidies will be necessary in order to get it into everybody's hands. However, there is no need for everybody to have this technology at first, only those people who are particularly worried about identity theft and who can afford to cover the cost. In all likelihood, even with mass-produced tokens instead of software, the overall cost to an end user should be well under $25, even for early adopters carrying the cost of the entire supply chain. Over time, the cost should go down, allowing the government to more easily subsidize it for low-income families.

Identity theft is certainly a significant problem that the industry needs to address, but even though the costs would be high and the lead time would be long, the world is better off taking a long-term approach and trying to solve the crux of the problem once, instead of continually plugging small holes in a dam that is about to burst.

In a practical sense, I strongly urge the U.S. government to task NIST (the National Institute of Standards and Technology) to lead development of a national standard for a Social Security number replacement, and then mandate its deployment on a long-term roll-out schedule. If such an effort were to begin in 2009, it would be quite feasible to see a real solution for those who are willing to pay a modest fee for it by 2020.

CHAPTER 27

Virtualization: Host Security's Silver Bullet?

The biggest problem with host-based security has always been what happens when your protection fails. And yes, all traditional host-based protections will have the potential for failure, especially when you consider that it's generally easy to trick users into installing bad stuff.

But when your protection fails, and the bad guy has a foothold on your machine, you're in a very bad spot. The bad guy generally can, if he puts in the effort, disable any security product you are running on your machine. So even if your product of choice eventually does protect against a threat, it could be too late for you.

Often, when bad guys disable things, they don't disable all security products. If you're using a good product that isn't as popular, that can leave you better off than running something with a brand name that every bad guy in the world will want to target.

The security industry hasn't been able to overcome this problem in the past 15 years. I expect to see that change because there is a relatively easy solution to this problem—virtualization technology.

With virtualization, you can run one operating system on another. I don't mean that you have to be running two graphical user interfaces on top of each other, such as running Windows on Mac OS X. Instead, you could have a very small operating system that the user typically doesn't see. Just for the sake of discussion, let's call it SecureOS. This operating system would have your desktop operating system of choice running in it (for discussion, let's assume you're running Windows). In an ideal world, your security software could run inside SecureOS and be able to protect Windows. If Windows got infected, only Windows would suffer. That's because, from the Windows point of view, it is running on some machine and doesn't see that it's really at the mercy of SecureOS.

If a bad guy breaks into your machine without being detected by your AV or other host security software, he has still only broken into Windows, and not SecureOS. The AV software can still make a network connection from within SecureOS to get updates that would allow it to clean up your infected Windows installation after the fact. Right now, once Windows is infected, the only sure-fire way to make sure your AV (or other host security product) is doing its job is to download a boot-time scanner on a known safe machine, and then run it when rebooting the potentially infected computer. Even rebooting is too much of a PITA (pain in the [neck]) for users. With virtualization, the user doesn't have to do anything—it can all happen automatically in the background.

This scheme is technically feasible, though it is complicated to build. Particularly, moving all of your host security out of Windows would require a lot of work, because host security products generally rely on parts of Windows to run well, even if it's just the filesystem. However, there is a middle ground where some security code can run inside the OS if necessary, talking to the SecureOS. The SecureOS would monitor the integrity of the security code within Windows so that it could detect when the bad guys are tampering with it. Plus, the communications and update channel would always want to live outside of Windows.

Additionally, there's the issue of what happens when SecureOS is itself not so secure. That is, if the virtualization platform has a security problem, it could be possible for a bad guy to break in to it if he breaks in to Windows. However, there's far less of an *attack surface* here. That means there are far fewer doors and windows to secure than normal, which generally would make it less risky for you.

The same kind of virtualization technology can provide great protection for your personal data. Your personal data (particularly credit card numbers, Social Security numbers, and things like your mother's maiden name) need never leave SecureOS unless it is explicitly encrypted for the company you want to do business with. Your Windows machine would just be relaying some encrypted data, and wouldn't be able to see your personal information. Clearly, there has to be a way to enter and change your personal data in such a way that the user won't be confused as to whether or not it is secure. At the end of the day, that's a big usability problem, but there is no real underlying technological issue.

One of the key requirements for a system like this is having true boundaries between operating systems, with limited communication interfaces (i.e., a small attack service). There are solutions where things run *semi-virtualized*, meaning inside the operating system, but with a lot of trickery to try to make programs unable to see other programs running). Such solutions have some usability problems that will make it extremely difficult for these solutions to be any kind of silver bullet, and they also have a much bigger attack surface, since they really are running inside the operating system.

However, you could do this kind of thing at the hardware or BIOS level. Hardware-level support for virtualization helps bring this kind of technology closer to reality. And if Apple wants a real leg up over Microsoft, it should put this kind of technology into the Open Firmware, which it controls (in contrast, Microsoft does not control the firmware for the machines on which it runs, which makes its virtualization efforts even more important).

The major issue with this application of virtualization technology is the cost. Host security vendors would have to do a lot of engineering work to retool their technologies. Then they would have to get customers to consent to the virtualization. On new hardware with direct virtualization support, there wouldn't necessarily be much or any performance impact, but legacy computers would certainly have a big issue. Plus, even for existing hardware that does support virtualization technology, vendors would have to wrestle with people migrating their nonvirtualized OSs to a virtualized setup.

Nonetheless, I think virtualization is the long-term future of host security. Your main OS will eventually be virtualized as a "guest" operating system. Security services will start migrating into the "host" OS, which, I hope, will be a small, dedicated piece of technology.

If we can make it that far, the advantage in the never-ending war between security vendors and the bad guys will, for the first time, shift to the security vendors. Vendors will be able to make pretty reasonable security guarantees under reasonable assumptions. No longer will they have to cross their fingers and hope the bad guys don't get administrative privileges or find a way to break in to SecureOS, something that, as a specific and constrained piece of technology, will be fundamentally easier to secure than an entire operating system.

CHAPTER 28

When Will We Get Rid of All the Security Vulnerabilities?

There are two common ways for malware to get onto a machine:

- The victim puts it on there himself. This is usually unintentional, as in the case of downloading something like a screensaver that really has malware bundled with it.
- The user does nothing wrong, but the malware shows up anyway. This occurs because of security flaws in the software.

There are tons of security vulnerabilities in software. They're swarming all over the place. From 2005 until today, an average of over 7,000 vulnerabilities each year have been publicly disclosed in popular software. There are many, many more vulnerabilities than are publicly disclosed. Some are found and fixed, but there will always be many security vulnerabilities that are never found.

In some sense, we can try to make it as easy as possible for users not to screw themselves, but some people will always fall prey to legitimate-looking scams, so there will always be a problem. But my data suggests that more than half of all malware shows up when the user does nothing wrong. Then there are all the security problems in web applications that can put your data, if not your machine, at risk.

It seems like we should be able to do something about this problem. After all, can't the developers writing all the software fix it?

Frankly, I don't see software ever being free of vulnerabilities. Let's assume for the moment that we already know everything about how software might fail and be used for evil purposes (even though we don't). We still have a lot of problems:

- It isn't worth it financially to try to train everyone to be an expert.
- It really isn't possible to turn most people into secure programming experts anyway.
- There are no incentives for developers to spend time on security.
- There are no incentives for companies to invest enough in the problem.
- Even experts make mistakes and miss things, so we would have a hard time getting rid of all the problems.

There's a lot that can go wrong in software that a bad guy can exploit. Becoming an expert in everything that might possibly go wrong basically requires studying security and working only in security for a long time. For example, when you get into areas like cryptography, the technical complexities take a long time to master. To really understand that field, instead of just following some rules that a master of the field gives you, you need a deep, graduate school–level of understanding of lots of obscure mathematics.

Most of the people who are "secure programming" experts don't even have a deep understanding of cryptography. The guidance on cryptography in many secure programming books is flat-out wrong and will lead to the creation of programs a bad guy can attack. Heck, there are several cryptography books where that's the case.

The point is, it's never going to be cost-effective to fill people's heads with all the knowledge they need to avoid security problems. Even if computer science classes devoted one class per semester for the full four years of college to the problem, it wouldn't be enough.

Yes, there's a lot of material to master and it's hard to absorb all of it. But more than that, there are plenty of people who will never absorb any of it. In the late 1990s I did a lot of security consulting and spent plenty of time in large development organizations in a variety of industries. There were always one or two people who were enthusiastic about security, but didn't have time to learn. But approximately 3/4 of the people I'd meet had no passion whatsoever for technology. They would generally leave work at 5:00 p.m. and do the minimum (but little more), because they saw their jobs as a paycheck, not something they enjoyed. People like that are unlikely under any circumstances to have the passion necessary to master the depth of security problems.

But even the people who could learn all the material and might actually enjoy it have no real incentive to become security experts because their companies don't reward security expertise. This is partially because it's tough to measure that kind of expertise, and partially because many companies have little incentive to care about security, since their customers don't demand it.

In a typical development organization, developers are measured on schedule accuracy—whether they get stuff done on time. When you look at the typical schedule, the focus is on the features that customers want. In some organizations, security tasks might actually make it into the schedule, but they're usually not the top priority—if something else is slipping, security tasks might get cut.

And if the task is, "review the code to try to find security bugs," how do you measure success, and how do you measure quality of effort? If the developer comes back and says, "I didn't find any security bugs," there may not be any, or there may be dozens, even hundreds. Either way, it's difficult to tell whether the developer did a poor job or a good job. Even if there are dozens of bugs, maybe they're all extremely obscure and require a level of expertise the developer doesn't have.

One way you might think to address the problem is with tools that try to find problems automatically. Some tools like this exist, but there are entire classes of security problems that such tools aren't ever going to be able to find by themselves—it will always take a human to find them.

Even when trying to get developers to do preventive things, it's often tough to measure whether they're actually doing them. And, if they don't do them, they're more likely to be rewarded with bonuses because they're more likely to meet their schedules.

And what happens if someone finds a security vulnerability in the product later on? The organization deals with the problem, but

I've yet to see anyone get in trouble for it. Perhaps the company will try to do better on a shoestring budget, but even if it fails, nobody takes any blame.

The philosophy is generally that the developers aren't security experts. Even if they've spent a lot of time in training and are making best efforts, they are probably not immune from accidentally leaving behind security problems.

I think that philosophy is right. Even well-respected security experts have accidentally left security holes in their software. It's too much to expect the average 9-to-5 guy to be anywhere near that good, especially when there's so much he'd have to master to make a real difference.

It's pretty rare that companies have to deal with security issues, relative to the number of problems that are likely lurking in their code. Let's say there is about 1 security vulnerability per 10,000 lines of code. I've done this study a few times over the years. There are a lot of variables, and the number can get a lot better (if you're Dan Bernstein), or a lot worse (if you're the average C developer), but this is a good enough guess for our purposes. Let's say there are only 10 billion lines of code in the world in production (there are probably a lot more than that, as many commercial applications have a few million lines of code).

That would lead us to believe there are at least a million security vulnerabilities out there waiting to be found. Last year, however, the public only heard about 7,000 of them. Over the lifetime of the Internet, we are unlikely to have found more than 2% of the security vulnerabilities out there.

If you've got security problems, but nobody on the outside world is going to find most of them, then it generally doesn't make much sense to spend money trying to eliminate vulnerabilities. For most small businesses, it probably doesn't make any sense at all, because people on the outside world aren't likely to target their software.

If you're Microsoft or Oracle, you're going to be a big target, and if people find enough vulnerabilities, you might get a bad reputation for security (as happened to both those companies), which not only impacts your brand, but can ultimately lead people to your competitors. There, you might care.

What about in the middle? Well, let's look at a well-known soft-ware company that we won't name. For about 10 million unique lines of code, it has had about 40 vulnerabilities found over the lifetime of all its products (many of them not even serious, so only a handful that really could impact its users). Since most of its applications are written in C or C++, I would expect it to have more like one vulnerability per every 2,000 lines of code. If we assume these guys are following all the best practices, they might be able to get down to one vulnerability per 5,000 lines of code. Well, it should have at least 2,000 vulnerabilities in its software. If that's the case, the outside world has found 2% of the vulnerabilities we would expect to be there.

To get its good security reputation (relative to most companies), this company spends less than $1 million a year on making its products more secure. Remember, this is a company with practices I'd consider to be above the industry norm. If this company were to have any hope at all of finding all the bugs in its software, it would have to spend a lot of cash.

Look at Microsoft, which has spent billions on this problem, done a great job of tackling it, and hasn't come close to keeping all the security problems out of the software it releases. The security company Secunia released 71 advisories in Microsoft products in the first 10 months of 2008. In all of 2007, they released only 69. Advisories often refer to multiple similar bugs found at the same time, so in each of the past three years, Microsoft has had over 100 vulnerabilities in its vast software portfolio exposed to the public. Microsoft really started spending a lot of money on the problem in 2002, so six years and a couple billion dollars later, it hasn't come close to eliminating the problem.

In fact, a massive amount of the development effort for Vista was in securing it. Microsoft went around and touted Vista as the most secure operating system ever. Yet, in 2007, the first full year Vista was out, there were still 36 public vulnerabilities announced, just specific to Vista. Granted, that's better than the first 12 months that Windows XP was out, when there were 119 announced (and not all of them were fixed in that year). But Windows XP didn't benefit from the security spend. Vista benefited from about $1 billion in spending, and only saw a 70% reduction in first-year vulnerabilities.

This seems like a losing battle. Let's say that Microsoft had done no work on the problem, and the year-one bug count was twice XP's. Instead of spending $1 billion on overall improvements, it could have budgeted $1 million for each of the 238 expected vulnerabilities, with the money going to fixing each problem as quickly as possible and getting the fixes out. Most of the cost manifests itself in schedule slip, and probably just would have been absorbed without spending. But let's say Microsoft would have spent that $1 million anyway. That's still less than 1/4 of the amount it actually spent.

Again, I do think it made sense for Microsoft to spend all that money, because it had a very real brand problem due to the bad security of XP. But, if you're any other company (well, except for maybe a big financial company or a government agency), the cost of "doing it right" is far higher than the cost of only responding when someone does find a problem, and other companies are unlikely to be risking brand damage.

Look at Apple. People often find security vulnerabilities in the products, often dozens at a time. And while the security industry knows this, the world sees Apple as a more secure platform.

Security problems in software have come to be expected. Customers don't even blink any more. You have to be large, or a security vendor, to face any risk of brand damage.

It's reasonable to expect the industry to do better, but only if there are cost-effective approaches to the problem, with an easy way to measure success and compliance. That's a future that's very far off, and even if we get there, you can still expect plenty of security problems to plague software.

CHAPTER 29

Application Security on a Budget

This chapter was coauthored with David Coffey, Director of SiteAdvisor and Product Security at McAfee.

A few big companies like Microsoft and Oracle have had enough security problems in their products that they've made massive investments in application security. For instance, the two of us frequently hear that Microsoft has invested at least $2 billion on the problem since about 2001.

Most companies aren't so lucky (or, should we say, unlucky?). It's tough to argue for budget, because, in most cases, it's difficult to determine the value of product security activities. Here are the most important factors that will get people to spend time and resources on security:

Compliance
> Some standards, like PCI (the payment card industry standard maintained by Visa), do require some product security activities in order to be compliant. Similarly, some customers, particularly parts of the U.S. government, may have requirements that software security work be done, such as external audits.

Brand
> Frankly, software users are desensitized to security flaws. Most companies can handle a lot of security flaws without

any real consequences for the public. Microsoft, Oracle, and big security companies are the exceptions, not the rule.

Customer demand

Sometimes customers do expect some security, particularly security features. For example, customers may occasionally ask for SSL support in an application.

Feature parity

If another product has a feature like SSL, competing products will often scramble to achieve parity. This is generally feature-driven, but if some product made lots of marketing hay out of external audits, their competitors probably might invest in them as well.

Assumptions about cost savings

We have seen some organizations with a track record of problems make investments in activities on the assumption that there will be a positive return on investment. For instance, we have seen development organizations spend money on training, just because they suspect there might be problems in their own code.

It's not too often that development organizations invest in secure development just because they want to make the customers safer. The general philosophy is, if there's no demand, why do it? There are more cost-effective things to do with time, particularly giving the customer things they actually want.

When there is a bar set by a customer or through some compliance mechanism, you can also bet that most organizations will be looking to meet the bar, not worrying about exceeding it—unless you can prove that it's cheaper to do a better job (which it can be if you invest in security early in a project, instead of after the code is developed).

In our experience, development companies will actually spend money on product security as a matter of course, driven by one or more of the reasons just described. Maybe it's that someone found a bug in the product and the company needs to respond, or it could be that all the competitive products out there use SSL, and there's a need for parity.

Our belief is that if a company is spending money on this problem, it is worth trying to make sure it gets the biggest bang for its buck. Often, if a vendor puts effort into a program, it will get better security for less money than it will if it deals with hot potatoes as it catches them.

We often hear from people from software development organizations who have problems, and are doing a little bit here and there but want to be doing something better, to be ahead of the curve. They ask us, "If I have little to no money to spend, what can I do?"

Our answer is that it depends on whether they are starting a new product or (as is usually the case) trying to make a positive change in an existing product.

Let's start with existing (legacy) products. Here's what we recommend for those of you with the same question:

Try to figure out what you're already spending
> The basic idea is that if you know what the organization spends, you can argue for more budget by saying, "We can make our software more secure by spending less money." We like to go around to all appropriate teams with a short questionnaire that tries to estimate how many hours a year are spent on security issues. This questionnaire should be done either in person or over the phone, otherwise you will never get people to respond. Also, it has to be short. We also think it's best if you use an outside firm to do this work, if possible, as that makes the analysis more objective. If done right, this exercise usually takes one to two hours per development team, plus a bit of extra time to tabulate data.

To try to prevent public vulnerabilities from coming out, steal the low-hanging fruit from the bad guys
> Since most software is closed source, the bad guys looking for vulnerabilities typically won't go further than using blackbox testing tools (this means they run the software and try to send bad data to it in hopes of getting it to behave badly; the primary alternative, reverse-engineering, is a heck of a lot more expensive). Bad guys typically use two techniques. First, they run web vulnerability scanners, which are commercially available and cheap. You can run these yourself and fix the problems they identify. The second thing the bad guys do is *fuzz testing*, which involves substituting random (but structured) data where real data would normally go into an application.

The cost of doing this yourself is usually easy to absorb, because development teams already have a QA budget (for our purposes, we will factor in the time developers spend fixing the critical issues found by QA), and these organizations are measured on bug counts and severity, not bug classification (e.g., security versus nonsecurity). The first time a QA organization checks these things, the bug count usually shoots up with extremely severe bugs. Plus, these kinds of tests are easy to automate. In the scope of a single project, we have found it's relatively easy to absorb applying 1/5 of your QA resources to security. In the long term (after sufficient automation and after the whoppers are fixed), the right ratio is 1/10. Again, if you can afford to get an outside organization to do this work, it should be more cost-effective than cultivating the expertise yourself.

When outsiders find vulnerabilities, handle them efficiently

When outsiders report vulnerabilities, they usually expect to go public with the information. Internal responses can be chaotic without a good process (an owner who "cracks the whip" over people to make sure they keep response a priority). In organizations without this capability, it's very common for researchers to go public before a vulnerability is fixed, just because someone at the vendor dropped the ball. This often ends up costing a lot more, because you still have to do all the same things to fix the problem, plus you may very well have to spend a lot more time dealing with customers who want to understand their level of risk and your company's response. We have found that small to medium organizations without processes generally spend at least $20,000 of people's time in the development organization. That's before any of the support costs. In our experience, the overall costs go down by about half when you take a structured approach (more of a savings in support than development, but still some hours saved). Remember, this is a cost you'll end up incurring no matter what—the issue is how effectively you manage that cost.

Cultivate security advocates

Few people on a development staff will ever care about security. For those who show any sort of passion (but no more

than about one person per product, and one QA person for
every four products), we think it is worth having that person
take the lead in doing research and making recommendations when it comes to security features. If you pick good
self-starters and give them responsibility, you may get a bunch
of extra work out of them.

*Hook up tools that enforce security style in development
organizations*

You can easily make sure that new code doesn't contain
"risky constructs" by hooking up your version control system
to a tool such as RATS (*http://www.fortify.com/security-
resources/rats.jsp*) or Flawfinder (*http://www.dwheeler.com/
flawfinder/*). This requires only a day or two of development
work. We recommend disallowing changes, as opposed to
auditing them. Developers will quickly absorb costs because
they will fix these issues as they come up, just like any other
warning their programming environment puts out. And, they
will quickly learn how to change their habits to make the
tools you use shut up!

For *greenfield* (from scratch) development, there really is no need
to do an organizational analysis. Instead, the single most important thing for this kind of development is to do *an architectural
risk analysis*. If you can ensure your program is designed with
security in mind, the long-term cost of security is very likely to be
much lower. Some well-trained third-party organizations will do
this kind of audit for you in a couple weeks for only about
$20,000. If this process can help you design away even one bug
that bad guys otherwise would have found, then this pays for
itself. And, most commercial products will end up with easy-to-
find flaws in the cryptography if they don't go through a process
like this, even if they use SSL!

For the remaining items in our list, we recommend doing the same
things for greenfield development.

For both types of development (greenfield and legacy), if you find
you have a bit of support from your higher-ups and can get some
cash freed up, we also recommend doing the following:

Measure your progress

If you know how much you have been spending, it's particularly useful to show whether you really are saving money. And you should always be able to report on the progress you are making. How much did it cost you to respond to an outsider's security bug this time versus last time? How many security bugs are you finding per dollar spent? When you're getting started, you want to see how well you're doing by comparing this to representative outside organizations. When the number starts jumping way up, it could very well be time to stop spending money on finding bugs.

Train security advocates

These people are generally eager to learn and will find ways to apply their knowledge, even while continuing to complete their existing responsibilities.

There are a couple of things other people might recommend that we *don't* think should be a top priority:

Code auditing

In our opinion, this is not a very cost-effective way to find bugs, even when you're paying for tools. Not only is it expensive, but also the bugs you do find with code auditing often won't be the same ones the bad guys will find. As a result, even if you're finding lots of bugs, it's tough to show the value of an audit because you might not have gotten the stuff that the bad guys will find most easily. And again, it does tend to be expensive. Commercial vendors can charge $.50 per line of code or more.

For in-house development, even if you have highly skilled people (which are extremely hard to get, whether you hire them or grow them), it's tough to do a good job and spend much less than $.10 per line of code. We would expect a phenomenal junior auditor making about $60,000 a year to be able to review about 400,000 lines of code per quarter with assistance from third-party tools. Typically, this process generates a large number of bugs, and then it is costly to prioritize them, figure out which ones to fix, and then go do all that work.

Note that unless you want to spend even more money, it's generally tough to tell whether you're finding bugs that bad guys could exploit, or just regular old bugs. Most companies are going to find it *vastly* more cost-effective to do QA testing and then fix other bugs as the outside world tells you about them.

Development team training

When you consider the direct cost and lost productivity, it typically costs about $1,000 a day to train a developer. It's well established that classroom retention rates (without lab work) are generally around 50%, even immediately after the class. We have found that most developers don't care much about security and consider even basic software security stuff "very complex" (which it can be). Therefore, retention rates are probably even lower than that. We've seen some data indicating that developers, on average, will have forgotten over 90% of secure programming training after six months. We think these numbers are about right. It's not worth it. Just train the ones who are excited about learning—they're the only ones likely to do a good job for you, anyway!

There are other activities you might consider, especially when you start getting down into the development weeds. Some of these additional activities could be important, depending on context. For instance, development teams may choose to use particular security technologies, and there is a cost to choosing, learning, and using those technologies.

Note that while code auditing and training are at the bottom of our list, we still think they can be valuable, and there is enough budget to get them done (and done well) at McAfee. We just think everything else provides far more bang for the buck. But if your primary driver is selling to the government and it needs you to get a code audit done, then code auditing will obviously jump to the top of your list. Our list is just based on what tends to be most cost-effective.

One question we often get is, "How much should an organization spend on product security?" We think that it's definitely possible to do on a tight budget. We've seen that medium- and large-size software development houses (say, companies with hundreds of millions in revenue) tend to be doing a good job if they're budgeting as little as .25% of their annual engineering budget on product security (people doing bad jobs often budget nothing at all). Software shops in financial institutions and the government probably want to go higher than that. Small companies that actually care about the problem typically budget about 5–10%.

At a very small company (i.e., one that has little revenue or has just started to make money) resources are at a huge premium. So, if you're going to spend at all, we recommend a small, fixed-cost investment for some third-party architectural help if it's greenfield development. Otherwise, just deal with stuff as it comes in.

We think the industry needs to make it easier for development shops to justify spending. It's incredibly difficult to prove the value of preventive labor. It should really be possible to compare your spending and your results against your peers.

We think that governments such as the U.S. government (or other organizations that own compliance regulations) should insist that companies that want the government's endorsement (selling into the government or PCI certification) provide them with data on their secure coding practices, for the sake of aggregating and publishing for free. No single company's data would be put on display, but companies would have a yardstick to measure their own activities.

Especially when data crosses the whole industry, it will be far easier to see how to regulate various industries for the sake of compliance. This suggestion is far less invasive than mandating code audits from third parties, and ultimately far more valuable to the world.

CHAPTER 30

"Responsible Disclosure" Isn't Responsible

I was pretty amused recently when two people I respect went at each other over vulnerability disclosure, quickly devolving into name-calling. It's always fun to watch a flame war (nobody got compared to Hitler, but one person did get compared to senile old Grandpa Simpson, walking around with his pants down).

But, to some degree, the two guys seemed to be talking past each other. One was arguing that full disclosure (meaning that vulnerabilities in other people's software will be made public eventually, no matter what) puts end users at risk, and the other was arguing that finding and fixing bugs is an important part of keeping code secure.

I happen to agree with both of them. Yes, if we didn't have good guys finding and fixing problems in code, there would be all the more problems for bad guys to find and leverage in their quest to take over the world. This is particularly the case because many development organizations don't invest in fixing problems, since there aren't good incentives (plus, there isn't much of a talent pool for this kind of work).

But, most of the problems in software that bad guys leverage are problems that the good guys have found and publicized.

If we hold to these two arguments, it seems that we can either live in a world where we hide our security problems but are at risk from bad guys easily finding lots of them, or we can live in a world where the good guys hand the bad guys a roadmap for how to be bad on a silver platter.

In the "keep it secret" model, how are people protected? First, we can hope that it is difficult for bad guys to find security problems without source code. Second, we can hope that the software vendors try to keep the security problems out of their code in the first place. Finally, we can hope that when the bad guys are leveraging problems in the real world, it will quickly get back to the vendor and the vendor will want to protect people.

In the "let it all hang out" model, security flaws in software are made public. Usually, the vendor gets a few months of advance notice, so hopefully people are protected with a patch that we have to hope they will install in a timely manner.

In the real world, both of these models have their advantages, but still pretty much suck because they leave people vulnerable.

Also in the "let it all hang out" model, the bad guys will prey on the fact that most people don't keep their software up to date. They will then take the flaws that the good guys find and use them to attack systems that aren't patched. This puts the burden of security on the end user. And, because there are thousands of security problems disclosed every year (often in important software), people are constantly at risk. Bad guys try to leverage flaws quickly before people patch, and they assume that, soon enough, there will be more flaws they can exploit, thanks to the good guys.

In the "keep it secret" model, vendors often won't find out about flaws when they're being used in targeted attacks. And, because people don't hear about specific security problems, it's a lot harder to put pressure on vendors to spend money to fix them. In this world, there are a lot more security problems out there (not as much investment in finding and fixing), yet the bad guys have to do a lot more technical work to find the problems they can exploit, so they are unlikely to be as profitable in leveraging security problems. They will either need to spend a lot more money to find software flaws they can exploit, or they will hold on to the flaws they have and only use them in targeted attacks.

You might say the first scenario looks better because we should rely on people to keep their systems up to date. However, we know that even people who are well educated on the issues often don't patch in a timely manner. That's just a reality we have to deal with. And it's a rational thing—there are some good reasons for it:

- Users might want to make sure updates are stable before they install them. Nobody likes it when an important program stops functioning properly.

- A user might not be entitled to the update, because he or she is using a version that is so old the vendor doesn't support it anymore, and that person doesn't want to pay for something newer.

- It may not be clear that there are security implications for the update. Certainly, some geeks assume that any update removes security problems (though, if new updates have lots of new code, maybe there are actually more security problems rather than fewer). Most people don't have the "always patch" mindset.

- The risk is perceived to be low. Even I will admit to going for days without installing Apple's OS X security updates because I feel that I'm not engaging in any risky behavior, and because my machine is protected by other measures (e.g., NAT). Of course, I realize there is still some risk (e.g., a malicious ad, which is why I tend to update my browser immediately when it has security problems). Whether wrongly or rightly, people feel pretty safe on the Internet in general (if that weren't the case, there would be much more demand for more and better security).

The fallacy in comparing and contrasting these two "sides" is in assuming they constitute the only options. In fact, they don't. The "keep it secret" model is the world we lived in 10–15 years ago. The "let it all hang out" model is the world we live in today. But I envision a better world.

To figure out what we should be doing better, you'll find it instructive to look at the history of vulnerability disclosure (at a very high level), and see where it's failed.

Back in the early 1990s, not too many people cared about their software having security flaws, mainly because few people were on the Internet. There were some people on local Windows networks in the workplace, but few people worried about the insider threat coming electronically because there were more direct ways to compromise a network.

Yet, researchers were starting to figure out that software could have security flaws, and that those flaws could have disastrous consequences, particularly that bad guys could, if circumstances were right, take over a machine from the other side of the world, remotely running whatever code they liked.

At that time, researchers were generally pretty altruistic, meaning there weren't too many economic incentives keeping them from following their own interests over the greater good. They didn't want bad guys to use these flaws, so they tended to contact the software vendors to tell them about the problems they found and how to fix them.

Most companies just ignored people reporting these security flaws, or dragged their feet indefinitely, promising fixes where none were forthcoming. Companies typically aren't altruistic. Sure, they wanted their customers to be safe, but they didn't want to incur the cost of understanding and fixing the problem (many security researchers vastly underestimate the impact on development costs). From the point of view of the company, customers weren't demanding security. And they didn't see too much risk, because the good guys were the only ones who knew about the problems. Sure, the bad guys might find out about a problem, but until there was evidence that they had, it seemed reasonable to do nothing. Many people assumed the bad guys would never go looking, or that if they did go looking, they probably wouldn't find the same particular problems (which is an interesting issue I won't discuss further right now).

The good guys didn't like leaving people at risk, so by the end of 1993, some people decided that they'd try to force vendors to do the right thing by threatening to disclose their problems to the world if they didn't fix those issues.

This approach actually worked. Disclosure helped build awareness. In particular, disclosure of flaws in Microsoft products caught the attention of some tech reporters, who not only put pressure on Microsoft to fix its bugs, but also eventually gave Microsoft a bad reputation for security due to the sheer volume of problems.

This doesn't mean everything has gone smoothly. Some vendors have felt blackmailed, believing that disclosure put their customers at risk. This is particularly the case when vulnerabilities are disclosed before the vendor gets a chance to fix the problem and get the fix into the customers' hands.

As a result, most people in the vulnerability research community eventually decided "full disclosure" was probably not the right thing. They shifted toward "responsible disclosure." This term might mean slightly different things to different people, but in general it implies that vendors will get advance notice of a problem, and two to three months to fix the problem and get the fix to their customers.

That sounds a lot more reasonable, but there are still a few problems:

- While 60 or 90 days might seem like a lot to a vulnerability researcher or even to some developers, for those on the business side, who look at all the things that need to happen to get software to consumers, it can often be too little time.
- Even if the vendor can move in 90 days, it's unreasonable to think that customers will upgrade in that timeframe.
- If the vendor actually fixes the problem, why the heck should the world be told about it anyway?

Let's look at that last point in more detail. The people on the disclosure side would say that if problems are not disclosed, fewer people will patch because they won't know they're at risk, but the bad guys may look at what's changed to figure out what vulnerabilities the patches address. On the other side of the argument, disclosure increases the likelihood of exploit for people who do patch, because the bad guys are told for sure that the patch fixes the problem, and are even given a good idea of what the problem actually was. When problems are silently fixed, with those fixes rolled into a regular release along with lots of nonsecurity-related code updates, the bad guy doesn't get much of an idea of whether there was anything wrong.

Plus, even if there is disclosure, it's very rare that the average consumer will notice the security risk (it basically needs to be reported in the press or similar media). And, people who are well versed in IT should already assume that every patch might potentially contain security fixes.

At the end of the day, this question boils down to, "How much does disclosure help the bad guys?" The answer is, "A ton!" In its most recent Global Internet Threat Report, Symantec reported that it had detected 15 zero-day vulnerabilities in 2007, meaning it found 15 vulnerabilities being exploited in the wild before the vulnerabilities were disclosed to the public. But, according to the Computer Emergency Response Team, there were at least 7,236 vulnerabilities disclosed in 2007.

I haven't seen any explicit numbers published, but the vast majority of malware that leverages security flaws (easily above 95%) uses vulnerabilities that are public information.

Of course, that doesn't mean that no one sits on undisclosed security flaws. I know plenty of people who do, including the U.S. government. But bad guys tend to use such security flaws very cautiously in hopes of keeping their weapons effective for as long as possible.

At the end of the day, if we stopped disclosing problems once vendors fixed the issues, the bad guys would find more vulnerabilities themselves, yes, but we'd be making it far more expensive to be bad.

All evidence I've seen indicates that if a vendor is going to fix a problem, disclosure is a bad thing for the average software user. So, why does it still happen?

The short answer is that the vulnerability researchers want the fame, fortune, and glory. The economic interests of this community are no longer aligned with the interests of the end user. Individual researchers want to get their names out there so they can make more money. They can also sell vulnerabilities. Legitimate companies, like TippingPoint, will buy the vulnerabilities. Then, such companies will disclose those vulnerabilities to the world. Doing so gets them attention from the security community, so this is effectively a marketing strategy. Plus, by purchasing vulnerabilities, they can provide their customers with protection before they release the vulnerability, whereas other vendors will usually need to wait until the vulnerability is disclosed before they can protect their customers. The vendor that bought the vulnerability can then argue that it protects people against more stuff faster, because it can find problems and protect its customers before public disclosure. So, companies like this are making people far less safe in order to market themselves.

Wasn't the purpose of disclosure to make people safer by forcing vendors to fix problems in their software? Microsoft fixes problems as soon as it can, and yet people insist on giving the bad guys the keys to the kingdom. As an industry, we've certainly lost sight of what's important.

I think the industry should move to the following disclosure practices, which I will call "smart disclosure":

1. When a good guy finds a security vulnerability in a product, he contacts the vendor through standard means (generally, by mailing *security@domainname.com*).

2. The finder gives the vendor 30 business days to confirm the problem and produce a schedule for future action. The finder will provide any support needed to confirm the problem.

3. The agreed-upon schedule should, at the very least, have dates for when a fix will be implemented, when a fix will be fully tested, and when a fix will be made available to customers. Unless the vendor can reasonably justify its workload and priorities, the fix and the testing should each be scheduled to take no longer than 90 days.

4. The parties should report progress on a weekly basis for the first month, and then at least monthly thereafter.

5. If the next scheduled product release is 4–12 months out from the day of confirmation, the vendor should be allowed to roll the fix into that scheduled product release.

6. If the next scheduled product release is fewer than 4 months out, the vendor should be allowed to roll the fix into the subsequent product release, as long as it is no more than 10 months after the impending scheduled release.

7. If there is no scheduled product release, the vendor should have six months to make a release.

8. If the vendor does not provide a schedule (within the specified time constraints) within the 30 days, the finder should give two weeks' notice, and if the vendor still does not provide a reasonable schedule, the finder is free to disclose.

9. If the vendor is not dealing in good faith, and if any part of the schedule slips 60 days, the finder should give two weeks' notice for the vendor to complete any past due milestones. If the milestones are not completed in those two weeks, the finder is free to disclose.

10. If a problem is being exploited in the wild, the vendor must acknowledge the problem and provide its schedule to the public.

11. For the first 18 months, the vendor's wishes on disclosure should be respected. If it wishes to allow disclosure in conjunction with the patch, it may. If it wishes for the bug to not be disclosed, it may. If the vendor does agree to disclosure, it must acknowledge the finder's role upon disclosure.

12. Eighteen months after the fix is made generally available, the finder may publicly disclose the problem. The vendor must acknowledge the finder's role at this time. Typically, this is done when publishing guidance about the security flaw to the customer base.

The bulk of these guidelines revolve around scheduling and communication. I have found that most vulnerability researchers do not understand the ways in which large software development shops tend to operate, and have unreasonable expectations on when and how fixes can happen. I've also found that most software vendors don't know anything about the security side, and don't know how to keep the finder happy, so the finder should be able to point to "smart disclosure" and the software vendor can then see what is expected.

The last two items are, by far, the most critical. I put the last item in there because I realize that the vulnerability finders are doing a good thing, even though the primary reason they do it is for the publicity. We still need to keep the marketing as an economic incentive in there, but we want it to be far enough out that people who are reasonable about updating will be protected. We should then encourage software vendors to give security warnings when people are running software that is more than a year behind in updates.

For people who are fervent proponents of "responsible disclosure," there are a few more objections they might have to my logic:

Many companies such as Microsoft are supportive of responsible disclosure

> The security industry today, as a culture, has already taken for granted the notion that "responsible disclosure" is good. A few people have argued this notion, but on the whole, people seem to assume that since it's better than the nondisclosure days, it is right. But when you get outside of the security community, do you really think that product managers are happy about disclosure? It hurts the reputation of the product and company, while putting the product's users at risk. They might not complain too loudly, for fear of looking bad if they get called out by the press for "not caring about security." I think it is mostly irrelevant what companies think anyhow....

Shouldn't companies be required to let their users know when there is a problem, at least when the patch is issued?

> As an industry, we have learned to take it as a given that software has security problems. Even if you've removed all the ones people have been able to find, there are probably more waiting to be found. As long as a problem isn't in the hands of a bad guy, it seems to be in the user's best interest to not know about the specific problem, because if he doesn't know, the bad guy is less likely to find out.

But won't the bad guys just reverse-engineer your patch and find the security issues?

> If security fixes are rolled into an actual release, where there are tons of other changes, generally not. Note that the software industry does this all the time with security bugs that are found by internal audit. They silently fix the problems they know about, and it is very rare to see disclosure of such vulnerabilities (though it does occasionally happen—I'd say from experience that it's far fewer than 1 in 100 fixed security problems, and it is almost always the case that the bugs are disclosed years after the patch). Now, if the release is explicitly a security-enhancing release, the bad guy *will* reverse-engineer it and find the problems. They won't be masked by thousands of innocuous code changes. That means if Microsoft keeps up its "Patch Tuesday" tradition (they release security fixes for

their software one day a month, on a Tuesday), it absolutely should keep disclosing.

What if we disclose the problem at a high level, but not in enough detail to reconstruct the problem?

If you tell people there is a problem and give them a general sense of where to look, you've cut their costs tremendously. Look at what happened when Dan Kaminsky found a major bug in DNS last year. Once Daminsky acknowledged there was a bug, trying to get people to patch in advance of the disclosure, a small segment of the vulnerability research community went off and rediscovered it and published it to a blog. The bad guys went off and did the same.

While I do think smart disclosure is the right way to go, I also think the culture we have today is pretty ingrained and will be difficult to change. Particularly, I don't expect that Microsoft would stop Patch Tuesday. First, it's not in the economic interests of the vulnerability community to delay taking credit for finding vulnerabilities, so even though it's hurting end users, it is unlikely to be supportive of any improvements. Since the vulnerability community will be evangelizing to the security community and beyond, there is a good chance that if Microsoft tries to move from a monthly patch model to practices based around smart disclosure, there will be a backlash. The vulnerability researchers will try to paint Microsoft as *not* caring about security, even though it's doing the best thing for its customers. Heck, I'm sure that there would even be plenty of people within Microsoft who are so indoctrinated in today's security culture that they'd also disapprove of a move away from Patch Tuesday.

Therefore, I don't really expect anything to change. I hope it does, and I'd like to see governments legislate disclosure practices that are in the best interests of their people, or something like that. However, I do want to emphasize to those of you who aren't caught up in the culture of today's security industry that the industry is doing you a huge disservice. Particularly, the many companies that find vulnerabilities as a way to market their own security products (a list that even includes big names such as IBM) are giving tons of ammo to the bad guys and making the world a less secure place for the rest of us.

CHAPTER 31

Are Man-in-the-Middle Attacks a Myth?

About seven years ago, someone I know proved to me that you could get pretty much any software you wanted for free, if it was sold through PayPal. All a bad guy had to do was copy the web page that sold the software and change the price on it. Then, when the bad guy clicked on his own malicious copy, it would go back to PayPal. If the vendor didn't use a special PayPal system (where PayPal connected to the merchant over SSL to confirm the transaction), then PayPal just trusted that the price was real.

I don't know about now, but back then nobody really used this system. And if they had, it wouldn't have made much difference, because unless you were a big cryptography geek, you'd be using the PayPal sample code. And, I noticed that PayPal's code didn't show how to secure the SSL connection properly. If you followed PayPal's lead, it would end up being easy to perform a *man-in-the-middle* attack on the connection (I'll give a brief explanation later for those who don't know the term). I pointed all this out to Max Levchin, founder and (at the time) CTO of PayPal. He didn't seem to believe it was a real issue, and certainly didn't think it was important, because none of his merchants seemed to care about security. Citing merchant apathy is a fair response, actually.

And then the original guy who contacted me decided to get the story some press coverage, and a *Wired* reporter was soon calling me for comment. I told him what I knew, and he wrote an article about it.

Levchin was also quoted in the article, and in it he claimed that being able to perform a man-in-the-middle attack against PayPal's underlying payment protocol was "highly improbable," reiterating his belief that such an attack wasn't practical. This from a guy who the article claims is an "expert in cryptography." I can't consider someone an expert if he's totally unrealistic about how practical a man-in-the-middle attack is.

Very briefly, what is a man-in-the-middle attack? Let's say you'd like to connect from your computer to some server using cryptography. If both sides aren't careful about checking each other's identities, they might end up talking to each other but not directly. An attacker could be sitting in the middle, relaying (possibly changing, or even dropping) messages. Everyone still talks using cryptography, it's just that the legitimate participants assume they're talking only to each other, but they don't check to make sure.

Levchin seemed to believe that man-in-the-middle attacks were only theoretical because an attacker would have to go upstream to your ISP or some major router between you and your destination in order to get in the middle. Levchin believed that ISPs tended to keep their routers pretty secure, by limiting who could access them administratively. Routers have a ton of traffic going through, but Levchin thought only the administrative traffic put end users at risk. Despite the fact that the Cisco router operating system IOS has had plenty of security issues (and many were known even back then), I do agree on that point. Attackers aren't generally going to want to break in to routers, because it is very tough to do without causing a noticeable impact on performance. If you're an attacker, even with a zero-day IOS exploit, I'd guess that there are much more cost-effective things to go off and do with your time. I think most people see this, and I've met a lot of people who take this conventional wisdom and conclude that man-in-the-middle attacks are essentially a myth, that they're not really something to worry about in practice.

Wrong! As it turns out, man-in-the-middle attacks are really easy to launch, using a technique called ARP poisoning. I'll spare you the technical details, but in a nutshell, a bad guy can use ARP poisoning to trick machines on a local network into thinking his machine is the local gateway, meaning all users send their traffic through the bad guy's machine to get to the Internet.

There are plenty of tools out there that can help launch these attacks pretty easily, such as DSniff, ettercap, and Cain & Abel.

All a bad guy needs is a foothold on somebody's LAN. If the guy in the office next to you has been infected and is a botnet node, you are probably on the same network, so some bad guy could launch man-in-the-middle attacks against you, no problem. Home users on cable in the same neighborhood tend to be on the same LAN. So, if you are running an eBay business from your house and you're using PayPal's IPN code direct from its website, it would be easy for a bad guy to leverage a neighbor's machine and attack you.

Your code, taken from PayPal, would try to connect to PayPal's servers, but the attacker would intercept it and return a "Yes" response, no matter what the transaction. The bad guy could then claim he'd paid you, but the money wouldn't be in the account.

I don't know for sure if people have really targeted merchants using PayPal. It's certainly possible. But, I do know that bad guys will launch man-in-the-middle attacks in the real world and use them to snoop plain-text passwords going to email servers, IM servers, and the like. They will sometimes even attack SSL sessions and scrape out passwords and credit card info from the transmission. These things can happen and can put you at risk, even when your computer doesn't have any infections.

ARP poisoning attacks can be detected, and high-end hardware from Cisco and others has been doing detection for a couple of years now. That's something an ISP might be able to use effectively right now, but the feature needs to trickle down into low-end equipment. And even then, it will be a long time before a large percentage of the world swaps out its equipment. Please, network vendors, bring this feature to all hardware, ASAP!

Once that happens, ARP poisoning attacks may become more or less extinct. But even if we can get rid of them, there's actually a much worse class of man-in-the-middle problem. Wireless devices are often susceptible to man-in-the-middle attacks—for example, when you go into a coffee shop and connect your computer to the wireless hotspot. Let's say you go there every day and connect to the hotspot, which is called, conveniently, "CoffeeShop." How do you know when you get online that you're really talking to the coffee shop instead of some bad guy? It turns out that, if the bad guy can produce a much stronger signal than the official signal, you'll see his network, not the original.

Similarly, if a bad guy wants to eavesdrop on an encrypted home network, he could just set up an unencrypted network with the same name, and the user probably won't notice the difference. And, believe it or not, similar attacks are possible with most cellular phones (though cellular attacks do require expensive equipment).

Yikes! What can you do to protect your wireless connections? For cellular calls, there really isn't much that's worth doing. It's too expensive to launch this attack for most people to care (since the average person is highly unlikely to be at risk). But for connecting to wireless routers, you should do something: make sure that, when you're connected to a wireless router, none of your sensitive data leaves your computer unencrypted.

Unfortunately, that can be challenging. Here are some things to keep in mind:

- If you're going to enter personal data onto a website, make sure the padlock is on, and make sure there were no error windows that popped up. In addition, click on the padlock to make sure the certificate is for the site you expect (bad guys in the middle can send you to their own fake site instead).

- If you're logging in to your home network (or a network you use all the time), make sure there is a password on your network. And, every time you connect, make sure you are connected with encryption. If you are, you're probably fine (generally, your computer stores the wireless password).

- If you're on any other network, don't use applications unless you know they're securely authenticating a server. For instance, the way many people have their email set up, it is susceptible to this kind of attack (and the bad guy might even be able to get their email password). Similarly, several popular instant messaging clients are susceptible to this kind of problem.

For now, bad guys can launch a man-in-the-middle attack on a machine that they've infected and collect useful passwords, all from the safety of an Internet café on the other side of the globe.

CHAPTER 32

An Attack on PKI

About three years ago, I was having breakfast with a friend of mine who was talking about a particular appliance product that claimed to be capable of transparently/silently intercepting all SSL/TLS traffic so that it could be inspected. He was asking me how this might be done.

In the SSL/TLS protocol, the client is supposed to validate the server. The server presents a certificate that is digitally signed, possibly with multiple signatures. The client is supposed to look at all the signatures and try to trace the lineage back to a trusted source so it knows all the endorsements on the certificate have been validated. To this day, many applications don't do this check at all, and just ignore the server certificate. Or they do insufficient validation of the certificate (for instance, looking to see that VeriSign has endorsed it, but not looking to see if it is the expected vendor's certificate).

Well, you can certainly do it if all the clients are set up to use SSL/TLS through a proxy server. Or, you could install a root certificate on all your clients and lie to them about who they're talking to. Or, you could just replace the valid certificate with one of your own, and most applications won't notice (though web browsers will generally prompt users with a security warning the first time they see the certificate). The appliance in question was probably taking one of these approaches. But it struck me that there was another, more devious way.

The trick is for a bad guy to start a certification authority (CA) that is tied in to the main hierarchy—the CAs that are already firmly rooted at the top of the PKI (public key infrastructure) trust hierarchy. CAs are trusted authorities who sign certificates for websites so that your browser can easily and securely validate that the data in the certificate is not fraudulent.

To start her own CA, a bad guy could go to other CAs and pay a lot of money for her own signing certificates. The certificates she signs would be endorsed by her. She wouldn't be known directly to all the client apps out there, but her credentials would be endorsed by another CA, perhaps one client applications do know about (and if not, somewhere up the line will be one that client applications do know about). This establishes trust with the client in the certificates she endorses.

What can a bad guy do if she starts up her own CA and gets it hooked into the main trust hierarchy like this? Let's look at what can happen if a client wants to browse to *www.citibank.com*, for example, and an attacker is in the middle. The attacker can generate her own certificate for *www.citibank.com* and endorse the certificate with her own CA, then present it to you. Your browser will validate it, and everything will look good, even though it is not the legitimate Citibank certificate. You won't get any warnings.

It's not all that hard to start your own CA, if you have the money for it. If a bad guy is going to do this, accountability is the big issue. She doesn't want to get caught. To start a CA, a bad guy will need to go through a validation process from one of a few small CAs that have the ability to bless a new CA, which (in an ideal world) means that the bad guy has to have a legitimate front. And she will probably have to meet people in person.

That's not an insurmountable obstacle by any means. Let's pretend I'm some nefarious foreign government, intent on spying on U.S. interests in this manner, or the NSA, intent on spying on nefarious foreign governments; take your pick. I would just get an intermediary to fund someone else to set up a legitimate CA, but keep enough access to the operation so I could get a copy of the signing credentials. I would set up some unsuspecting stooges to take the fall if something ever went wrong. Conversely, there are a few countries where I could register a corporation where the directors are anonymous. I could run a legitimate ISP in that country for a small while, then go through the CA process.

All told, it would cost maybe $150,000 to launch this attack. That's not a lot for a government or a computer mafia. And this all assumes that CAs that have the ability to bless other CAs are going to be doing their jobs when it comes to validation. In reality, there is a good chance things will be even easier to game.

Can anything be done to prevent this type of attack? You could hardcode the certificates you're going to accept or the CAs you're going to trust. Or, you could point out every change in a certificate. That is, if you've seen citibank.com before and you notice the change in CA, you could complain about it. But, frankly, if nothing else looks wrong, people are probably just going to click through any warning you give them. The bigger the potential user base, the more likely it is that there will be avenues for people to game the system. I'd rather see a lot of smaller, more definitive registries that have even more stringent audit requirements, like a registry of big financial institutions, and then local registries for smaller players, and similar structures for other industries. Or, even better (though probably less usable), people and businesses could establish direct trust relationships with each other. But that's just a pipe dream—any major changes to the way we establish trust are probably too big to actually happen.

That leaves the Internet fundamentally broken.

CHAPTER 33

HTTPS Sucks; Let's Kill It!

It's almost impossible to deploy SSL (and its successor, TLS) in a way that leaves everybody actually secure. SSL is great at providing a false sense of security, and not too much else. But, HTTPS (which is a variation of the HTTP protocol that enforces the use of SSL) is even worse, because it is impossible to protect everybody with it.

First, let's look at applications built using SSL. With most APIs, you can connect easily, with very little code, but the connection isn't validated. You just connect, and you have no idea who you're talking to. The server has even less idea. Usually you do some sort of login jig after that, but there's no guarantee that someone isn't sitting in the middle.

Well, maybe you're a smarter developer than that, and you do certificate checking. It's rare, but it does happen. Or maybe you're using an API that does some certificate checking. There are still a million ways to get shot in the foot. Many apps check to see that a server certificate is actually signed, but don't validate anything else about the certificate. Many apps check all the data in the certificate but allow self-signed certificates—hey, the bad guy can self-sign a certificate. Many apps give you the option to trust or even revert to no encryption if something fails, and people never expect that the worst will happen to them.

The makers of HTTPS were smarter than that. The HTTPS protocol specifies the validation that has to happen, and it is all the right stuff. Sounds great! Except there's a big problem: what happens when the certificate isn't valid? You get a lovely pop-up box that looks something like Figure 33-1.

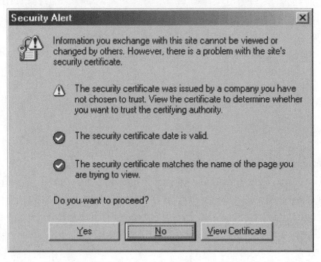

Figure 33-1. A standard security pop up shown when the system finds a certificate that isn't valid

Imagine your mother reading this. My mother is a smart lady with a Master's degree, and she would think it is gobbledygook. Most people aren't going to click No, especially if this dialog box keeps coming up every time they try a site. People don't want to be kept from their goals, and they generally aren't going to be too paranoid, especially when they get lots of dialog boxes they don't understand that seem menacing but end up amounting to nothing.

They might click View Certificate, but do they really know what they're looking for? If a bad guy was trying to attack Citibank, he could just self-sign a certificate with all the same data as Citibank's certificate, but make it look like Citibank is its own CA.

People will look at the data in the certificate, it will not seem fishy to any but the most seasoned of people, and most people will eventually click through.

This is particularly the case because most of the time you get a pop up like this, there is no attack in progress. It could be that an online web app you use has stupidly used a self-signed certificate. It could be that your bank didn't have its operations team on the ball, so its certificate expired (this absolutely happens). It could be that your employer needs to decrypt all your SSL connections for audit purposes, and then reencrypts, but they're all perfectly legit. The more sophisticated a user is, the more likely he is to have seen this dialog box in perfectly legitimate circumstances.

I'd love to run a study in which I could give some normal, middle-American mom and pop users a task, nominally to test the usability of the task in their actual bank accounts, and then serve up an invalid certificate. I'd like to see how many people actually clicked through the warning and logged in. I'd put down good money that the number would be well over 70%.

This is an utter, abject failure of the HTTPS protocol. The failure method ends up being "rely on the user." If I had designed the protocol, I would have designed it to never allow the connection if not everything in the certificate validated. The website is just inaccessible, period. If a bank forgets and lets its credentials expire, that bank should be down to the entire world.

This isn't a problem we can put back in the box. Let's say Firefox decided to report that "the site is down" whenever an HTTPS connection didn't validate. What would happen? Easy: people would try other browsers, and inevitably some people would switch to the other browsers due to the inconvenience. So there's no way Firefox would ever want to do anything like this.

Frankly, even if we spec'd out a version of HTTPS2 that was basically the same thing but failed properly, it wouldn't matter. There wouldn't be too much incentive for people to migrate.

For instance, if you ran a bank, unless it were regulated that the bank must switch, you would only be increasing the risk of your website going down eventually.

I think HTTPS could possibly be killed to make the world a better place, but it would need extra incentive, perhaps real phishing protection (which wouldn't be too hard to add). Maybe someday HTTPS will go away, but I'm not going to hold my breath, either.

CHAPTER 34

CrAP-TCHA and the Usability/Security Tradeoff

Over the past few years, most online signups have involved CAPTCHAs, perhaps the security technology with the worst acronym: *Completely Automated Public Turing test to tell Computers and Humans Apart.*

It's understandable that Google might want to see if it's a human signing up for that account or some automated program—bad guys would love to have lots of Gmail accounts to be able to send spam through.

Similarly, I can understand why ticket agencies like Ticketmaster might require you to confirm that you're a human before every purchase. Who wants ticket scalpers writing programs to automate buying tickets (well, besides the ticket brokers)?

But come on, don't these things make life horrible? I signed up for a Gmail account, which I use to look at my daughter's blog and post comments. Every single time I want to post a comment, I click Submit, and I get a pop up with a CAPTCHA, like the one shown in Figure 34-1.

Why the heck do I have to click two buttons (one to submit the comment and another to submit the word verification)??!! And it is a pain in the neck to type. I usually just don't bother commenting on a blog if I have to see one of these (though I do make an exception for my daughter).

Figure 34-1. *A CAPTCHA pop up*

The idea behind a CAPTCHA in this situation is to prevent bad guys from spamming blog comments. But is that benefit worth the annoyance?

At least Google's CAPTCHA is easy to read. Ticketmaster (which uses the popular reCAPTCHA package) can be a little harder to read (Figure 34-2).

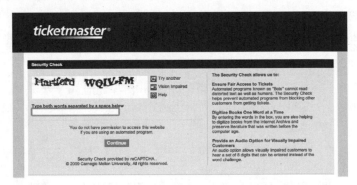

Figure 34-2. *The Ticketmaster CAPTCHA can be difficult to read*

Is that WQIV or WQLV? I'm not 100% sure. And, before the FM, is that a dash, a dot, or something I should leave out? At least there's a "Try another" button, because some bad CAPTCHAs just make you guess wrong first.

Figure 34-3 shows a particularly bad example (documented on zachfine.com) of a CAPTCHA found when trying to sign up for the Gizmo VOIP (voice over IP) network.

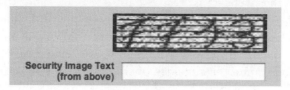

Figure 34-3. *Gizmo's almost illegible CAPTCHA*

Thankfully, Gizmo doesn't seem to use this any more. But still, there are lots of CAPTCHAs with cramped letters that are hard to read.

The reason for the cramping and distortion is to try to keep programs from automatically detecting the letters. That's a real problem for CAPTCHAs. Lots of real systems, including one Yahoo! used, have been "broken" so that it doesn't take a human to get the right answer, at least most of the time. Heck, bad guys generally don't care too much, even if the automation only works 1 in 10 times. That's still a lot of comment spam.

Let's say that researchers managed to come up with a CAPTCHA scheme that a computer couldn't break. It doesn't matter. Bad guys can just pay to have low-cost workers to fill in CAPTCHAs in real time. For example, look at the website shown in Figure 34-4.

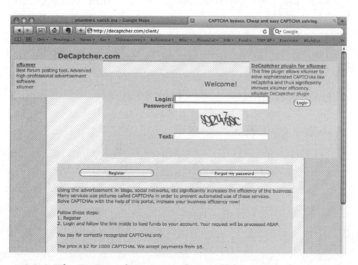

Figure 34-4. *The DeCaptcher.com website offers services for getting around CAPTCHA by paying other people to fill them out for you*

OK, so the website is really hard to read, and to request CAPTCHA-breaking services requires using one of the most awful CAPTCHAs ever. However, you can pay someone a mere $2 to break 1,000 CAPTCHAs. That's a lot of tickets if you're a ticket broker and want to buy a bunch of crap using your automation. All the CAPTCHAs will get entered in as quickly as possible by people in cheap-labor markets like India. The ticket broker doesn't have to do anything once his automation is set up.

If it's this easy to get around a CAPTCHA, they basically don't work, right? Why, then, are we subjected to a nightmare of usability for no good reason?

From the fact that people still implement CAPTCHAs, it's clear that this minimal bar is better than no bar at all. Big players like Google seem to believe that the bad guys would try to send a lot more spam if the CAPTCHAs weren't there. From a cost perspective, that might be true, if the fraction of a penny per CAPTCHA was near in cost to the average return on investment from posting the spam in the first place.

Plus, cost doesn't have to be the limitation. It could be that there aren't enough resources available to meet demand for CAPTCHA breaking. It could be that the spammers would make enough money that they would pay the price, and if there were 100 times as many people doing the breaking, there would be 100 times as many CAPTCHAs broken. If so, the supply would go up until the demand was met, and CAPTCHAs would become less effective still. Whenever there's a financial incentive to break one, expect it will be broken.

Still, the bar is not zero. CAPTCHAs do add some cost to the bad guy, which means that some bad guys won't find it cost-effective, where they might have otherwise.

CAPTCHAs do have some value in preventing bad stuff, but the problem for me is they are such an annoyance to the mass of legitimate users. Do we have to deal with a less usable experience to help offset the problem?

Or are there perhaps better alternatives that would make it so we don't have to see CAPTCHAs?

Well, it's possible to do some network analysis that tries to detect automation. It's usually easy to detect automation when lots of connections are coming from a small set of addresses, but it could potentially be tough to detect automation coming from a large botnet.

To have a hope, one has to look at what connections actually do. For example, Google would have to do spam detection on comments. Generally, that kind of detection can be very expensive (though Google does search blog comments for spam anyway).

That kind of scheme is expensive. It certainly would work better, but I suspect the economics aren't too attractive.

I'm fine with that, but what I'm not fine with is the way vendors ignore usability. Like I said, Google making me fill in a CAPTCHA every time I comment on my daughter's blog, when I'm posting as myself (i.e., not anonymously), makes me not want to use Google blogs. I hope other people feel the same way.

Couldn't Google at least just require the CAPTCHAs for account creation and then throttle me if I start posting too many comments? It seems like it would be better for Google to make its customers' lives less miserable.

I'd like to see the CAPTCHA mostly go away, which would be possible if we added more accountability to the Internet. One type of accountability is an identity service. For example, VeriSign sells credentials for websites that show up in your browser as a certificate when you're doing SSL. What if VeriSign gave away personal identities (actually, it already gives away email certificates), and if you allowed it to hold verified personal information about you and a credit card that was occasionally checked for validity, you wouldn't ever have to see another CAPTCHA. If your account was used to spam or was found to be cheating when buying tickets, your agreement would be that VeriSign could come after you for damages. In my mind, VeriSign shouldn't necessarily be allowed to charge to a credit card. It just must be possible for it to identify you and sue you.

This system would also be a good single sign-on mechanism. I wouldn't have to create new accounts on every new website if they were all tied into this system.

If we had a system like this, most of us would be able to go about our lives without having to see another crappy CAPTCHA. Or, if you don't care about the usability but you prefer your privacy, you can skip identifying yourself and just go with the CAPTCHAs. Either way, at least there would be a choice.

CHAPTER 35

No Death for the Password

Passwords suck. There are all sorts of problems with them:

- Simple passwords may be easy to remember, but they're also easy for automated systems to guess.

- Lots of people use one or two passwords for all their accounts, or have similar bad password practices that increase their risks.

- If you try to do the right thing and use different passwords everywhere, it's easy to forget important passwords, particularly the ones you don't use often.

- If you use a program to remember your passwords, you now have one very important password. When you need to log in from a friend's machine, you might be in trouble. And you can be in a horrible position if you don't keep backups and your computer dies.

- If you use a program to remember passwords and you leave your computer unattended, people may be able to just sit down and access your accounts.

- In many cases, your passwords can be snooped when you use them. It could be malware running on your computer and logging your password, or it could be malware on your coworker's computer, looking for passwords on its way to the Internet.

- Passwords make it risky to use other people's machines to access the Internet, because who knows what kind of keylogging malware is installed? For instance, when I go to a conference or into the Apple Store, they often have machines for accessing email, but I refuse to use any password.

- Password recovery systems often increase risk. It's not tough to find out my mother's maiden name or to find the name of Paris Hilton's dog.

- It's easy to socially engineer people out of their passwords. For example, if a bad guy claims that he's from Harvard and is doing a study on computer security (particularly, on how good people's passwords are), a lot of people will give up the password in the name of science, without calling Harvard to find out if the study is real.

- It's tough for systems developers to build a system that eliminates unnecessary risk. I won't go into any technical depth, but one important point is that there are a bunch of places where usability and security trade off. For example, eBay doesn't want a bad guy trying a few million times to guess somebody's password, so it might set a limit of 100 login attempts per day. But then, it becomes easy for a bad guy to lock people out maliciously.

With all that said, it's difficult to see anything killing the password. First, there aren't lots of great alternatives. Sure, there are things like proximity badges and fingerprint scanners, but those things are expensive and don't always work as well as they should.

Second, it's much better to improve security by combining authentication techniques. By that, I mean you have to jump multiple hurdles before a system will accept who you are. This is called *multifactor authentication*. A simple and common example is getting cash out of an ATM. There are two authentication factors there. First, there is a pretty weak password (your PIN). Second, you need to have the ATM card that matches the account from which you want money. Bad guys can't try to attack bank accounts just by saying whose account they want and then trying some PINs.

That's not to say we can't make password systems more secure. There are lots of things we could do.

First, systems that need to use passwords would be far more secure if they used something called a *zero-knowledge password protocol*. In traditional password protocols, bad guys can do tricks to guess a lot of passwords quickly. Zero-knowledge password protocols remove every avenue for the bad guy to learn more about a password than through random guessing. When equipped with this protocol, systems need to protect only against excessive guessing. Zero-knowledge password systems aren't often used, however, because of a patent minefield that has been a big impediment to standardization. Thankfully, important patents start expiring in 2010.

Second, instead of (or in addition to) traditional passwords, we can use one-time passwords. One-time passwords are a pretty old idea, and lots of corporations use them. The technology most people are used to seeing is the RSA SecurID, which is a physical device people typically hang on their keychains. The device shows a new six-digit number once a minute. While SecurID devices are expensive, it's trivial to make a good one-time password system that is totally free.

For example, I've built a system called OPUS that works like this:

1. On the web page or program you're logging into, type in your username and click Send Passcode (Figure 35-1).

Figure 35-1. Logging into the OPUS security system

2. A randomly generated password is sent via text message to the phone of the person who has that username (Figure 35-2).

3. You enter the passcode in the web form (Figure 35-3).

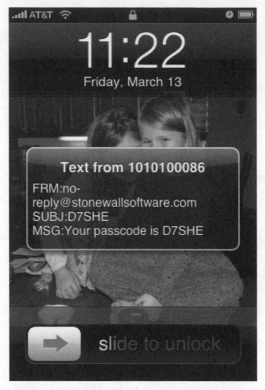

Figure 35-2. A random passcode is sent to your phone

Figure 35-3. Entering the passcode

For more security, you could have a private four-digit PIN, which you also need to enter alongside the password.

There are lots of technical details under the hood to help make a system like this secure. But, for people who are interested, I've made the OPUS system freely available at *www.zork.org/opus/*.

The great thing about this system is that you don't have to remember passwords anymore. You just have to keep possession of your phone, just like you would with your ATM card.

That's all well and good, but even though the computer industry can do better than it does today with password security, you can bet passwords will continue to be an important part of security systems.

Yes, it's important to protect yourself from people guessing your password. You should assume that it's not just people who know you who might be trying to guess it; anyone might be trying to. Assume the system you're using is weak, and it's up to you to have a strong password.

For instance, let's say I have an online account with the *Old York Daily Times*. You may not think there's any real value to getting a password from an online newspaper site, but I still used a moderately difficult password. But what if its system is poor, and a bad guy tries 10,000,000 guesses on my username before getting my password? The bad guy can then try that username and password combination on tons of other sites, like maybe Gmail or my bank.

So, please assume that you are at risk, and take a bit of responsibility to protect yourself by making sure your passwords are as safe as reasonable. Here are my recommendations for dealing with a world that is full of passwords:

- Make sure that, at the very least, important accounts have their own passwords. Even if you insist on one throwaway password for accounts you don't care about (such as newspapers), make your online banking password as strong as possible.

- A reasonable way to use one password across multiple sites is to vary your password for each site in a way that is consistent enough for you to remember. For instance, if your base password is "something", your Yahoo! password might be "something5Yo" (because Yahoo has five letters, starting with "Y" and ending with "o") and your Google password might be "something6Ge". This isn't a perfect scheme, but it's a lot better than using the same password for each site.

- If you don't want to have to remember more than one password and you keep your computer backed up, you can use a password storage application. Some of them will create very strong passwords automatically and fill them in for you, so you don't even have to know your own passwords. For example, if you use Firefox, there's a great plug-in called sxipper (*www.sxipper.com*). The only password you need to know is your password for logging onto your computer. If you use a system like this and you think you might need to use another computer, you can look at the passwords and copy them down or save the password database to a flash drive.

- Use passwords that are hard to guess, even if you have to write them down. Some security experts say not to write down your passwords because bad guys can find them under your keyboard. Well, just keep them in your wallet or purse, then. Or maybe on your phone. But you're better off with a strong password than a weak password, even if you have to write it down to remember it.

- If you're having a hard time coming up with a good password that you can actually remember, think of a favorite song lyric that is at least eight words long, then take the first letter of each word, along with any punctuation. And don't be afraid to make clever substitutions. For example, you could take the Pink Floyd lyric, "Money, so they say, is the root of all evil today!" and turn that into the password: $sts,itroaet!

- Another option that results in much stronger passwords (but might require you to write them down) is to use a program to generate them. For instance, you can go to password-generating websites like *http://www.goodpassword.com/*.

CHAPTER 36

Spam Is Dead

In 2004, Bill Gates boldly proclaimed that Microsoft would solve the spam problem by the beginning of 2006. That was wrong, but maybe not as far off as some people might think.

True, most people are still seeing ads for Viagra and love letters from horny Russian girls, and getting business opportunities from Nigerian princes on a regular basis, but not too many of them. Most decent antispam technologies out there work about 98% of the time, but if you're getting 15,000 spams a day before your antispam filter has its go at it (this is the level of spam I personally receive each day), that's still about 300 spams showing up in your inbox. That's probably great for the average Gmail user, who only would have gotten about 100 spams in a day, and only gets 1 or 2 in his inbox.

Another problem with a lot of spam filters is that they will tag legitimate email messages as spam. When you're getting a lot of spam, you're not going to want to try to search it periodically to figure out what your spam filter got wrong. This problem is worst with the spam filters built into most email systems. If you use an email security service or a big security vendor, this still happens, but they tend to be a lot better about it.

Even though 15,000 pieces of spam show up to my personal email addresses on a daily basis, I use a spam filter that lets through less than one piece of spam per day. Here's what my system does (it is not unique to me, even though I wrote my own code):

- If I've ever gotten an email message from you (that isn't in my junk folder), you are on my whitelist and you can send me email messages.

- If I've never gotten an email message from you, an automatic system sends you a response, saying, "I haven't gotten the message yet." If you follow the instructions (replying to the mail or clicking a web link), I get your email message. Otherwise, it gets deleted automatically a few days later without me seeing it.

- If you've ever spammed me, you go on my blacklist, and I will never see mail from you under any circumstances. This is where my editor's email address lives. (I added this to see if he was paying attention!)

- When I have to give someone an email address on a website, I can make up a new email address on the fly, and once I make it up, all email to that address gets automatically whitelisted so that I can get important automated responses, like order confirmations. If I get too much junk to that email address, I can just turn it off.

- I do a lot of technical crap to try to determine when people are sending from fake email addresses. For instance, lots of spammers try to make mail look like it is coming from legitimate email addresses at PayPal. This technical crap only matters if a spammer happens to forge mail, as if it comes from an address that is actually on my whitelist. For example, if spammers tried to forge email from Amazon, Amazon is on my whitelist, so I'd want to detect the forgery when possible.

With this system, I get, on average, one piece of spam a day. And by that, I really mean one piece of junk mail. It's usually an ad from some online store that I actually gave a customized email address to.

Junk mail from vendors you've legitimately done business with is a much bigger problem for many people than unsolicited spam. One easy way to address that problem is to give sites you do business with a temporary email address. You could open a Gmail account just to do business with those people, then close it afterward. Or you could use Mailinator (*www.mailinator.com*), which lets you make up any email address ending in *@mailinator.com* you want, and then lets you check the mail that email address receives.

Email is only kept for 15 minutes, so this is not ideal if you might want to get a shipping notification or something like that. It's great if you want to sign up for a web bulletin board and want to make sure the site never contacts you.

Once every few weeks, an actual spammer responds to my automatic "Haven't gotten your message yet" email. Of course, he has wasted his time, and I get some smug satisfaction from that (if the day comes when lots of people do this, I will make them send a text message to some phone number that automatically handles the result, so that they have to pay physical money to get me to see their message).

Some email services are starting to take similar approaches. I think it's a decent strategy. The big challenge is prepopulating the list of good senders, which can be automated if you've got an archive of your email or an up-to-date address book. Some companies can even build a whitelist like this from the mail being stored in folders on an Exchange server.

But few people use a strategy like this. Fortunately, a lot of people don't get thousands of spams a day, either. Most people seem to get much less, maybe a handful to several dozen for an old email address that has been sold a few times.

For these people, cloud-based spam services should work really well. These are services in which spam processing happens remotely (in the cloud) instead of on your desktop. This can include smart webmail providers, like Gmail.

Gmail is a phenomenal example, actually. It sees lots of mail going to lots of people, and it can analyze trends across this base of customers. It can see the same basic content being delivered to thousands of people at a time (a good indicator that something is probably spam). It can see when a targeted mailing is sent to a user's junk box, and will then send the same message to the junk boxes of other users who received it. Similarly, when it identifies spam sources, it can block them.

This kind of cloud approach gets detections up while keeping false positives down. The false positives that do happen tend to be mass mailings that some people consider spam, but really are not. For instance, when you buy stuff online, you often end up agreeing to subscribe to an email list for ads, whether you notice or not.

If you don't want those ads, you might mark them as spam, as may many other people. A good vendor has to watch out for this kind of tricky situation.

Your solution doesn't have to be having your email hosted on Gmail, though. You can get the benefits of the cloud on a desktop client. That is, if your client is good enough. Many desktop clients use a set of rules that is only updated when you update the software. But some desktop clients can download new rules in real time, and that's a lot more useful. Companies with that kind of system usually collect a whole lot of spam in the back end (primarily by taking over defunct Internet domains and seeing what comes in).

The best of both worlds is being able to do sophisticated cloud analysis and seeing user feedback for spam. Companies that do both (as most big vendors tend to do) regularly end up detecting over 99% of all spam. For instance, when I hook my spammy inbox up to Gmail, it does very well. In a typical six-hour period, it let 10 spams through in about 980 messages, giving it nearly a 99% detection rate. The average user would probably only see one or two spam messages a day, if that.

The lesson here is that if your desktop spam filter isn't doing a good enough job, use an antispam service. For example, if you own your own domain, there are specialized services, such as MXLogic (*www.mxlogic.com/*), that will take care of things for you. Or, if you've already bought a security suite from a major AV vendor, you are probably already paying for access to an antispam service, and you should use it!

It may still be the case that 99% of the email messages sent to you are spam, but you should never need to see them. The worst problem is that you might miss an important email message because it lands in your spam folder. The spam problem is mostly solved, but this hurdle may never be addressed.

But, actually, I don't really want the spam problem solved. It's solved enough. If it were solved all the way, I'd lose one of my most useful excuses, "I'm sorry, I didn't mean to ignore you; your email ended up in my spam folder."

I'm happy to say, that excuse isn't going away anytime soon.

CHAPTER 37

Improving Authentication

Bank of America is the largest financial institution in the world. Lots of consumers, myself included, use it for online banking. It also cares a lot about security, and has been progressive in adopting technologies. But even though it has all sorts of great things going on security-wise, I don't like authenticating to its site.

One technology Bank of America adopted long ago is SiteKey, which I think is pretty close to valueless. The basic idea is that when you register for an account, you choose from a large library of images (Figure 37-1). The image you choose is your SiteKey.

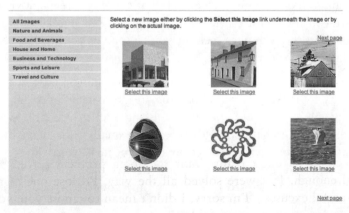

Figure 37-1. Choosing a SiteKey image

Then, when you go to log in later, here's what happens:

1. You type in your username.

2. Bank of America shows the SiteKey image you selected before.

3. If you agree it's your SiteKey image, you type in your password.

What's the point of the extra step? Bank of America wants you to recognize phishing sites, because it hopes phishing sites won't know your SiteKey. I suppose it hopes that the bad guy will pick a picture at random, and you'll know when you see the wrong one.

Maybe most people would notice and care if the bad guy selected the wrong image to show you, but, so what? There are two big problems here.

First, the bad guy can show you a phishing site that doesn't have a SiteKey at all. Most people probably won't notice, particularly because most sites don't use SiteKey.

Second, if the bad guy has broken into a computer on the network local to the user, he can quite possibly perform a man-in-the-middle attack, where you're actually talking to the bank, but the bad guy sees everything, including your username and password. In this scenario, SiteKey could show you the right thing, but you would still be talking directly to the bad guy.

Of course, if the bad guy has broken into the endpoint computer that the user is on, authentication mechanisms are moot, and the bad guy can do anything. One trick that bad guys are employing is to let you deal with the legitimate website, but inject new form fields onto the web page, asking you to type in your Social Security number for extra verification, for instance.

I don't see what SiteKey does, other than providing a false sense of security by making people think they're protected. True, the very few people who would notice the missing SiteKey probably won't be phished. In that sense, there's some small value here. But I don't think this extra protection mechanism is worth the extra login step. One sign that it's not an effective mechanism is that so few banks have adopted it. If it were any good, everybody would want to use it.

On one hand, the extra step isn't all that obnoxious. And at least Bank of America is trying, even if the security benefits are, at best, marginal. On the other hand, I am against it giving its customers an illusion of better security than it really has.

At the end of the day, I'm sure Bank of America won't get rid of SiteKey anytime soon. If it yanks SiteKey, it might receive criticism for taking away security measures.

Bank of America's online banking does offer a much more effective security mechanism it calls SafePass. The basic idea is that when you go to log in, it will send you a text message with a one-time password (Figure 37-2), which you then enter in to your computer (Figure 37-3). When I first saw this, I thought, "Now this is a great alternative to SiteKey!" I thought I'd be able to tell that I was talking to the real Bank of America, because a random phisher (hopefully) wouldn't know my mobile number, but the bank would.

Figure 37-2. SafePass sends a one-time code...

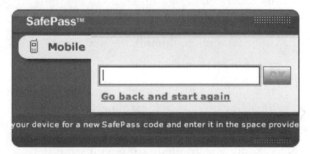

Figure 37-3. ...which you then enter in

Unfortunately, Bank of America really made the experience so intolerable that I turned SafePass off for logins. When I had it on, here was my login process:

1. Type in my username.
2. Validate my SiteKey.
3. Type in my passcode.
4. Wait for the SafePass widget to load (which can take anywhere from 2 to 10 seconds).
5. Click the button to send the text message.
6. Wait for the text message to show up.
7. Type in the code that showed up in the text message.
8. Click OK.
9. Wait a little more while the system finishes the authentication process.

I lived like this for a few weeks, but decided it was just too many steps, and too slow. Now I have SafePass configured only to take the place of security questions if I want to log in from a new device.

I have to think that if they could get me to use SafePass for every login, they'd be less susceptible to me being phished. And while I think I'm far more likely to notice a missing SafePass step than a missing image, that's not even the reason. If I'm successfully phished for a password, and I don't use SafePass, the attacker is far better off than if he also needs to get a hold of my mobile phone!

True, if the bad guy wants to log in to my account from a different machine and I don't use SafePass, he does need to know one of the answers to my challenge questions. Let's look at some of my 30 options for questions:

- What's your maternal grandmother's first name?
- What's your father's middle name?
- In what city were you living at age 16?
- What is the name of your first niece/nephew?
- In what city were you born?
- In what year did you graduate from high school?
- How old were you at your wedding?
- What was your high school mascot?
- What was the name of your first pet?
- What is the name of your best man/maid of honor at your wedding?

Almost all of the 30 options for questions are things that are public record. The rest of them are things people could typically find out without attracting much attention, if they had the right personal relationships. To counter that, you could always make up fake answers to all of these questions. The problem is then remembering the fake information, and also remembering which companies have the real information and which have the fake information. I just write all that stuff down.

Currently, Bank of America is effectively discouraging me from using SafePass by making the login process so complicated to use. Instead, it should be doing everything in its power to get me to switch to it.[1]

If I owned Bank of America, here are the changes I'd make:

- I'd encourage people to use SafePass by giving them value in return for using it. For instance, no fees, higher interest rates, or a nickel per check card transaction. It should be easy for me to figure something out that is valuable to users but costs less than the expected loss from not using it.

- If users are using SafePass, get rid of SiteKey.

- If users are using SafePass, don't make them type in their passwords.

- When the SafePass text message comes, Bank of America should do more work to prove that the one-time password is really coming from Bank of America, to assure me I'm not getting phished by someone who happens to know my phone number (this is particularly important if I get some notification to log in to my account via SMS). Bank of America could do this by sending a secret string to users to help identify it as the sender. This is basically a text-based "SiteKey" or a password in reverse (Bank of America sends you a password to prove who it is, instead of you sending one to it).

---

[1] By the way, I don't mean to pick on Bank of America too much. It really does seem to have the best security of any bank. It does plenty of effective things lots of banks don't do, such as authenticate the devices you log in from, and offer real-time server-side attack detection. I am only picking on Bank of America because I like it enough to use it as my bank. I have also talked to the team there that owns its consumer security initiatives, and they assure me that they're working on lots of improvements, and that includes making SafePass fast.

If I know to always expect Bank of America to send me a text message with a secret string, I'll never get phished. But the bad guy could still be doing a man-in-the-middle attack. If he does, however, at least he won't get a password that he can use to log in again, since he doesn't have my phone. Most people reuse passwords across sites, so that's another thing he won't be getting.

For extra security, you can always add a second password, one that the user types in. Then, a bad guy would need the phone and the password.

I would like to see phones used for authentication like this more often. I can imagine no longer having to carry around my SecurID because I have my phone with me (which would save the company money, by the way). I would like to see a day when I can go to a website and specify the blocks of time when I want my house sitter to have access to the house. The house sitter's phone could use Bluetooth and an application to prove he's there and ready to come in (hit the button to open the door). Or maybe the door lock has a small keypad, and the house sitter could text my door, and my door would text back a four-digit code to punch in to the keypad.

In short, it's possible to have systems that are easy, cheap, and pretty safe. Let's hope to see them someday.

CHAPTER 38

Cloud Insecurity?

One of the biggest buzzwords in technology these days is "cloud computing." The basic idea behind the cloud is that stuff that could be done on the client side gets moved to some unseen cluster of resources on the Internet.

There are three major categories of cloud systems today:

Software-as-a-Service (SaaS)
> In SaaS, you buy a subscription to some software product, but some or all of the data and code lives remotely. For instance, Google Docs is an alternative to Microsoft Office that stores your documents on Google's servers, and you don't keep any code on your machine. As it turns out, though, some of the code may run on your machine. For instance, Google Docs relies on JavaScript that runs in your web browser. The application is not hosted on the server side.

Platform-as-a-Service (PaaS)
> From the consumer's point of view, the software is probably SaaS, but instead of the software developer building the program to run on her own web infrastructure, she builds it to run on someone else's platform. For example, Google offers a service called Google App Engine, which allows development organizations to write programs to run specifically on Google's infrastructure.

Infrastructure-as-a-Service (IaaS)

> This is very similar to PaaS, except that the development orga-
> nization gets to define its own software environment. It basi-
> cally provides virtual machine images to the IaaS provider,
> instead of programs, and the machines can contain whatever
> the developers want them to contain. The provider can auto-
> matically grow or shrink the number of virtual machines run-
> ning at any given time so that programs can more easily scale
> to high workloads, and to save money when resources aren't
> needed.

From the end user's point of view, there's usually not much of a
difference between these three models. The security of the system
is dependent on things that are mostly out of the user's control,
such as:

The security of the IT environment from outside attackers

> For example, can the bad guys break in to the backend sys-
> tems and get at data?

The security from within the environment

> Can someone use a flaw in an application to see data for
> other users, or mess with other applications hosted in the
> same environment?

The authentication and encryption methods used

> Plain-text protocols with passwords put everybody at risk.

In this case, the IT environment isn't something the software
developer has much control over, either. The cloud provider needs
to be upfront about its policies, and application developers need
to do what they can. For instance, when using infrastructure-as-a-
service, it's best practice to create a virtual machine image that has
no unneeded functionality running, and to have instances use
encryption to talk to each other, just in case another customer of
the cloud provider might be able to intercept at the network level.

One significant advantage of all types of cloud systems is that if
the system is well designed, all the interesting code that a bad guy
might want to exploit will live on the server side (instead of being
downloaded to the browser). If the bad guy can't get hold of the
code, he can still attack it, but he has to leverage the flaws obvious

from the user interface or use brute-force testing techniques to find the problems. Those techniques are easy for the good guys to do, too, which makes the application easier to defend; you can find the flaws before the bad guys do.

Compare that situation to a typical architecture in which you can buy a copy of the server-side application to host in your own network environment. Anyone can buy the application, including bad guys. And, while the vendor typically won't ship source code, the bad guys will at least have access to the binary code, which they can read (though not as easily as if they had the source code). In a SaaS model, access to the binary code for server-side components should be extremely limited.

It's still possible for developers to put important things on the client side that should be on the server side. The developer has to assume that bad guys will have complete access to everything on the client, no matter what kind of obfuscation he does. For example, if the client is responsible for constructing and validating database queries and the server executes them blindly, the bad guy will always be able to modify the client-side code to do whatever he has permission to do with the backend database. Usually, that means he can read, change, or delete data at will.

Because the attacker has so much less information, I think it's quite justifiable to get away with an incredibly modest application security program. The exact scope really is dependent on the software developer's specific requirements, but for many organizations the cost-effective reality is, "Hire someone to do fairly cheap security testing," invest some modest resources in the authentication/encryption stuff everyone obviously should be doing, and quite possibly nothing else. You can most likely skip stuff like training and code review altogether if nobody is making you do them.

Whenever I get up and suggest caution about spending on application security, there are often people who are shocked because I've coauthored so many books on that topic, including the first, *Building Secure Software* (with Gary McGraw; Addison-Wesley Professional). I've been getting that reaction from people when talking about application security in the cloud.

And yes, this approach is demonstrably not going to lead you to the most secure solution possible, but business is about maximizing profit, not security. This is the right place to set the dial on the risk knob for most companies doing business in the cloud.

Of course, there are several use cases for which this advice may not apply. For instance, if your company deploys its solution in the cloud but sells the same code base on-premises, the bad guy has access to your code again.

Beyond the generic concerns of the cloud approach, each of the three cloud computing models has its own security concerns:

- With *SaaS*, users need to rely heavily on their cloud providers for security. The provider is the one who needs to do the work to keep multiple companies or users from seeing one another's data without permission. The provider needs to protect the underlying infrastructure from break-ins. In addition, it is generally responsible for all of the authentication and encryption. It's tough for the customer to get details to help provide assurance that the right things are being done. Similarly, it's tough to get assurance that the application will be available enough.

- With *PaaS*, the provider may give some control to the people building applications on top of its platform. For instance, developers might be able to do their own authentication systems and data encryption, but any security below the application level (such as host or network intrusion prevention) is still going to be completely in the hands of the provider. Usually, the provider will offer little or no visibility into its practices here.

- With *IaaS*, the developer has much better control over the security environment, primarily because applications run on virtual machines that are separate from other virtual machines running on the same physical machine (as long as there is no gaping security hole in the virtual machine manager). This control makes it easier to ensure that security and compliance concerns are properly addressed. However, the downside is that it can be a lot more expensive and time-consuming to build the application.

One more important concern is backing up data. Some providers do their own backups for you. However, lots of things can go wrong. Maybe they jack up their prices and make it tough to get data off their network. Sometimes companies suddenly go into Chapter 7 bankruptcy. Lots of things can happen.

In all cases, if you're using a cloud-based solution, it's best if you can keep your own backups of your data in addition to the backups from your cloud provider. This is generally far easier with IaaS.

The cloud obviously has a lot of advantages, such as cost sharing across companies (hopefully making it more cost-effective than having your own infrastructure), and helping to handle situations in which an application becomes popular and needs to scale quickly. But to many people, the cloud may feel more risky because their applications and data might live in some shared space alongside other applications and data.

Most of the time, however, bad guys have no access to the source code, and providers often do work hard to provide clean, unbreakable barriers between customers. Of course, security can differ greatly from application to application, from platform to platform, from provider to provider. But on the whole, the cloud holds a lot of promise for better security.

That's the good news. On the flip side, lots of people now have data and code on the same few sites—making those sites bigger targets.

The people who own these sites have to worry about all the same classes of problems that other development organizations have to worry about—but the consequences could be much worse because there could be a lot of people or companies with their data at risk.

People writing SaaS applications need to be worried about the application flaws that might show one customer's data to another, or expose data from multiple customers. Infrastructure-as-a-Service providers have to worry about making sure their customers are protected from one another; if one of them has a security breach, the other customers shouldn't be at any greater risk than they were before.

Cloud providers need to care about getting security right. They are the ones who are going to have to shoulder the responsibility when something goes wrong.

Let's hope they get it together.

CHAPTER 39

What AV Companies Should Be Doing (AV 2.0)

I've talked a lot about what's wrong with traditional AV systems that makes them work so poorly. Now I'm going to share my vision of what security vendors should be doing, which we'll call AV 2.0 (even though we're all sick of *Whatever* 2.0). I've been working toward this vision for a bit under three years now, primarily at McAfee. While no AV vendor is all the way there yet, the big ones are starting to move in the right direction.

AV vendors traditionally have kept a big blacklist of bad programs. Instead, AV vendors should keep a master list of programs, and for each one, keep track of whether it's good, bad, or undetermined (the vendor doesn't have enough information to say).

There's not much reason to have big signature files on machines, or even to check traditional signatures. Instead, right before the computer runs a program, the AV software can ask the AV vendor, "Is this program safe to run?"

Now the AV vendors have to become a lot better at detection. To that end, the endpoint AV software should collect information about the programs people put on their machines, such as things like:

- Where are files installed?
- Which software vendor "signed" it?
- What registry keys and other resources do programs use?
- What other programs do programs install?

- What things do programs delete?
- Do programs do anything suspicious, such as keylogging?

This kind of information doesn't need to be sent for every program. Generally, it should be sent just for programs that the vendor doesn't know about.

The AV vendor can then use the information collected about a program to perform a central analysis across the entire user base to determine whether the program should be trusted or not. When you have lots of data about programs across a user base, it's pretty easy and cost-effective to figure out which programs are good or bad:

Ubiquity
  If lots of people have a program installed and the program never behaves poorly, it is probably good (though it is a good idea to recheck this assumption occasionally). If almost nobody across the user base has the program, it might be suspect.

Digital signatures
  Programs digitally signed by a trusted vendor with a good reputation are probably good, and programs digitally signed by a vendor who peddles spyware probably shouldn't be run.

Lineage
  If an installer is highly trusted (perhaps due to a digital signature), it's generally worth trusting everything it installs directly (things packaged in a separate installer are possibly partner bundles, and should not necessarily be trusted). Similarly, anything a bad program installs, and anything that installs a bad program, should be suspect. Also, if we got a program from a risky site, we might not want to allow it to run until we are sure it is OK.

Behavior
  There are lots of behaviors that are potentially an issue, such as keylogging, inspecting network traffic, and so on. It can be tough to tell on a single machine if behavior is bad or not, but if you look across an entire user base, things can become far clearer. For example, you might be able to detect patterns that indicate botnet activity. Or, you might look and see that lots and lots of people use that program, even though it has some keylogging functionality. (Yes, I'm talking to you, Skype!!)

To see how all this helps, let's think back to what the bad guys are doing today to make the lives of AV vendors difficult. Then we'll see how this new model can make things better.

Bad guys know that if they use custom-made encryption (or packing) solutions, they can automatically create lots of different pieces of malware from one original piece of malware (usually they randomize the filenames and all sorts of stuff to make correlation difficult). They create tons of work for the vendor by using automation to spread lots of malware instead of just a single piece. If the bad guy's automation is really effective, the good guys will be overwhelmed by the number of incoming samples and will have an incredibly challenging time writing a signature that applies to every possible version. That's definitely typical in today's world.

Let's say my vendor is collecting intelligence across its entire user base, and my computer's AV reports that *someprog.exe* has started up. Via cryptography, the AV software computes a unique identifier for *someprog.exe* that does not care about the filename. This identifier is sent back to the vendor. If the vendor has never seen this program or has seen it only a couple of times, it asks for some more information before it renders a decision. Our software might report some other useful information, such as the fact that it's not digitally signed and is encrypted (it's easy to tell if a program is packed or encrypted—it can be really hard to recover the original program, though).

Based on what we've seen so far, the vendor would say, "Don't run this." Why? If a program is packed or encrypted and nobody has seen it before, it is incredibly suspect, and almost always bad.

Vendors like Microsoft, and even vendors with small followings, like Dropbox, will never have to worry about their programs being falsely accused, because their installers are signed, and any good AV vendor will end up whitelisting the vendor. Or, for software vendors that don't sign their stuff but distribute off their websites, the AV vendor will see that the software is distributed from a highly trusted website, and will let the software run.

With just a rule like this, very little legitimate software would ever be stopped, but bad software would be stopped pretty readily. What kinds of things will the bad guys do to try to get around the system?

Bad guys may start digitally signing their applications (using legitimately obtained code signing certificates)

This will make bad guys more accountable, because they will have to provide some verifiable information to get one of these certificates, and the certificates cost some money. While a bad guy can easily generate thousands of programs, it's unlikely that he will be able to get and use massive numbers of code signing certificates. Some spyware vendors that live in a gray area of legitimacy already do sign the applications they produce. I don't think the economics will work out for the typical bad guy, though.

Bad guys may stop packing their programs

Traditionally, the value of packing was in creating more work for the good guys by creating lots of programs. This worked well because the good guys had no real way of figuring out how to prioritize their workloads. Which programs are popular? Which ones aren't? Well, now the good guys will easily be able to disregard most packed programs, since most of the time bad guys repack programs over and over again with slight, automatic variations so that they're spreading bazillions of programs that all do the same thing. Bad guys will probably need make their programs appear more normal by *not* packing them and by not creating tons of variants (because the same kind of filtering can work well even if the bad guys don't pack or encrypt). The end result will be that the programs the bad guys can get through the AV filters will be far more susceptible to analysis than today's malware. Keeping malware off people's machines will be a far easier task.

Bad guys will be even more intent on disabling the AV, so bad behaviors won't be reported

But the good news is that before malware runs, the AV vendor will already have information about it, where it came from, and what happened when it was installed. This audit trail will help identify the risky software automatically and quickly.

Bad guys may try to game the system

For instance, a bad guy might try to get her software marked as "good" by having tons of already-infected computers report information that makes the program look like it's good. For instance, this approach may make it look like a program is spreading at a "natural" rate for a while, then the bad guy can go for the "sudden explosion" that would be expected when a program gets some publicity and spikes in popularity.

The last two techniques are tougher to deal with, and could create a bit of an ongoing arms race with the bad guys. But we're already in a big arms race, where the good guys are losing. This approach will put the advantage on the side of the good guys. For example:

- If the good guys move the security outside the operating system, it won't generally be possible to disable the AV.

- Even if the AV is disabled, the system can automatically respond to protect uninfected machines, based on data that was collected prior to infection. This means having a good solution to automatically clean up an infected machine by rebooting and putting in a special cleanup CD/DVD. This is easy to do automatically, because it's easy to figure out what the bad stuff did to the filesystem and undo it (at boot time, the bad stuff generally doesn't get to run).

- We can do a lot to automatically detect when people are trying to game the system. Because all the logic lives in the cloud instead of in a binary on the desktop, it will generally be *very* hard for the bad guys to figure out what all the rules are. With traditional AV, bad guys test and test offline until they figure out what they can get through. But now, the AV system will automatically change based on what's happening across a large number of machines.

Even when a bad guy does manage to game the system, the industry will still be in far better shape than it is today. It will be far easier for the good guys to keep up with issues, respond to them, and get customers protected.

There are some questions about this approach I'd like to address:

Aren't false positives still an issue?

Yes, it will still be possible to block something that's legitimate. But popular stuff from major vendors won't have this problem at all. The false positives that people have to deal with will be for stuff that isn't very popular, and in those cases, instead of saying, "This software is bad," the AV provider can just say, "This software is suspect. We'll let you know when we confirm that it's safe to run" (see Figure 39-1 for an example). This approach will work well as long as most of the software that people actually use is being graded in a timely manner (and in a company with a large user base, there's no reason why it wouldn't be).

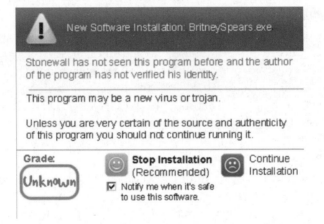

Figure 39-1. An example message about potentially suspect software

What happens when a computer is offline and can't query the AV company's server?

The computer's AV software will certainly remember which programs were good and which were bad. The only issue arises when running something unknown or installing something from disk while offline. In this case, the AV company can just cache a bunch of the most popular program signatures (this cache can be updated daily, just like signature files generally are today). For things not in that cache, they can just say, "You have to be online to ensure that this program is safe to run." Let the user override at his own peril.

Can't the bad guys make good programs do evil things by using exploits, and wouldn't that get around detection?

Yes. However, there are things we can do to address this problem. For example, we can look for behavioral anomalies on popular good programs that indicate they're being exploited. And once we know something is being exploited, we can certainly lock it down.

Doesn't this system raise a huge privacy issue?

Well, it's true that a lot of data about programs will be collected, but nothing that I'm proposing would send back your actual personal data. In fact, there's no reason why users would have to send back any personally identifiable information. And if this turns into a huge concern, the vendors could use an anonymization layer (which is quite feasible from a technical perspective). Plus, people should be able to opt out of data collection. Frankly, most people don't care about vendors knowing which programs they run or which websites they visit (and vendors will throw away this info, anyway), as long as a) there's nothing sensitive, like a Social Security number; b) the vendor is using the data for the greater good; and c) the vendor vows that it will never use the data for any other purposes. Heck, I think a lot of people really only care about the first point.

OK, but what about privacy for enterprises?

Some enterprises will care, but many will not. Those that do can stick with the traditional model and deal with far worse security. More likely, what will happen is that AV vendors will sell enterprises a big box that allows them to do their own data aggregation and analysis. They will still use data from their AV vendor, but they will have control over what they share. They will probably pay for that privilege.

Doesn't this increase network traffic?

Quite the opposite. Clients will generally only communicate with the server for programs they haven't seen before, and then, the data sent will be small in both directions. Today, every client gets massive downloads on a daily basis, many thousands of times larger than the data that this new system would send in an ordinary day.

There will be plenty of interesting directions in which the industry can go once systems like this are common.

For instance, this big database of all programs can have categories besides good, bad, and unknown. There could be subcategories for good, such as "exploitable" and "has known exploits," which can make patch management much easier. Imagine AV that tells you when you need to upgrade a piece of software because there are actual exploits for that software. Or imagine that your AV software could be extra cautious about allowing you to do risky things with exploitable software, such as opening attachments you found on the Internet.

We could classify programs in all sorts of ways. Certainly, we can have spyware or adware, but how about "crapware"? What if, when you tried to install a program, your AV software could tell you that most people end up uninstalling the program and that the program will slow down your machine (Figure 39-2)? What if it could make Amazon-like recommendations for programs before you run them or before you even download them?

Figure 39-2. An example "crapware" warning

There are plenty of other useful business opportunities to be built on top of a platform like this. But that's the future. When's the future coming?

Most of these ideas have been built, at least in a prototype form, but seeing them in production across millions of users will take a few years. The industry is moving with baby steps toward this vision, and it will continue to make baby steps because nobody wants there to be a disaster if some vendor goes out with something half-baked and causes problems. Vendors will make sure to build the right things. For example, the big vendors will need to make sure their solutions scale up to millions of users.

We're already many steps down the road. McAfee has been delivering some real-time signatures since mid-2008. And several vendors are tracking enough information about program ubiquity that they can at least start prioritizing their resources better. The major vendors and a few of the minor ones are typically doing some automatic reasoning about programs in the backend.

It will still probably take at least five years until most of this vision is reached. Even that might not be long enough for the industry to properly defend itself from bad guys disabling AV software when they do successfully infect a machine (that requires a virtualization approach, where the migration path is tricky).

But even when we get to this world we're envisioning, it's important to note that these systems are only going to make the problem manageable; they're not going to eliminate it. There will still be infections. There will still be all the things that lead to infection and data loss, such as social engineering and software exploits. There will still be network-level attacks to worry about.

But the world will be a much safer place, particularly for those people running AV 2.0.

CHAPTER 40

VPNs Usually Decrease Security

The basic idea of a VPN (virtual private network) is that people with the right credentials can get access to resources over the Internet that normal people can't see at all. What generally happens is that a machine connects to a VPN server and authenticates. That machine can then see both the Internet and the private network.

For example, many companies allow their employees to check work email from outside the office, but only if they VPN in. If an employee VPNs in, and that employee is infected, the bad guy on that machine suddenly can see a bunch of machines that just weren't visible before. Heck, maybe the bad guy will even commission some malware targeted to his victim's firm and its specific environment.

People get themselves infected. Why put your corporate network at unnecessary risk, just to give people access to email? Just outsource your email to a SaaS provider. Or run your own mail infrastructure, but lock it down really tightly in case there is a security flaw in the software.

VPNs made a lot of sense when most of the services people wanted to use didn't use strong authentication and all of a company's services ran on one network and had access to one another. But the world's not like this anymore. Most of the services corporate citizens use have strong authentication available, and you can either have that stuff hosted or otherwise segregate things far better than you could even five years ago.

Plus, VPNing is generally pretty damn inconvenient!

CHAPTER 41

Usability and Security

I've talked about this topic a few times in this book. Often, there's a tension between usability and security, where stronger security generally results in a less usable system, and a more usable system is often less secure.

I think this is a false dichotomy. It's certainly possible to have systems that are both easy to use and secure. For example, in Chapter 35 we talked about improving the security of password systems by applying a technology called *zero-knowledge password protocols*. Done right, implementing this type of system would also improve usability, because it would make traditional passwords far more secure than they are today.

There are plenty of other examples where security and usability go hand-in-hand. If you give users the ability to choose between a secure connection built on the strongest encryption that has provably strong properties, and something legacy that everybody's heard of (but might have security problems), plenty of people will choose the system they've heard of. Heck, if you give people the option to turn it off, some of them will. It's far better to have no options, and eliminating options also leads to the simplest user interface. Just give people a secure connection.

When it seems like security and usability trade off, there's a good chance that there's a much better solution that got ignored. Maybe the designer didn't take the time to look for it or maybe he didn't take the time to fight for it. Either way, everybody loses.

CHAPTER 42

Privacy

By now, people should have a reasonable expectation that there's no privacy on the Internet. If you want privacy, you have to read the fine print carefully to find out exactly what privacy has been promised and under what conditions. Most people don't think about it, and if they do, they don't care very much.

Many geeks, on the other hand, care a whole lot. Few of them know they're a tiny minority, though.

I think I'm pretty typical. I would love to have my privacy, but once you get past my personal finances and such (read: I don't want my money/identity stolen), I really only object at a moral, theoretical level. It's not a major driver for me, and I'm often willing to sacrifice some privacy for more functionality. I generally would not go out of my way to get more privacy unless I explicitly had something to hide. I almost never have anything to hide.

Most other people seem to feel the same way about it: privacy is nice in theory, but if you don't have anything to hide, what's the big deal? Maybe that's a shame, but it's the way the world is.

CHAPTER 43

Anonymity

Like privacy, anonymity sounds great in theory, but nobody cares in practice. A company called Zero Knowledge learned this the hard way when it offered a cool paid service that allowed people to use the Web anonymously. It worked pretty well, but nobody cared.

There are also significant problems with anonymity, such as the lack of accountability. For example, the night before I wrote this chapter, a coworker of mine had to spend a couple of hours dealing with police because someone out there used a VOIP phone to call 911, claiming to be my coworker.

Anonymity is a great ideal, but it's disappearing all over the place. You haven't been able to fly without an ID for a long time, but now it appears I can't even take Amtrak without having to show a government-issued ID. In one sense, that worries the hell out of me, but on the other hand, I do think accountability is important.

Oh, and I've got nothing to hide anyway....

CHAPTER 44

Improving Patch Management

Software has security flaws, as we well know, and we've seen a lot about why it can take time to get software fixed. But most of the time, fixes come out when a vulnerability is announced, and then the bad guys have a field day. Usually, they have at least a month in which they will have little problem finding people who haven't patched.

But why can't we get everybody to patch in a timely manner? After all, don't most programs these days include auto-updaters so we don't have to remember to go check for new software?

There are a couple of problems. In corporate environments, people like to make sure that patches are stable before allowing them to be deployed so as not to impact productivity. A security flaw that isn't being actively exploited, or one that presents a low risk (perhaps because users are mainly behind the firewall, or perhaps users are just expected not to open random documents from around the Net) may not be as risky as installing an unstable patch that causes the program to crash a lot, thereby destroying productivity across an enterprise.

The patching problem isn't just an enterprise problem. Normal people don't patch, either. I see my parents and friends go for months or even years ignoring their computers' cries for updates.

Heck, I don't patch often enough myself. I don't let things sit for years, but maybe a week or two.

The reason? Even if it's mostly automatic, patching is usually a big productivity hit. If I patch my web browser, I have to restart it, but at any given time, I may have 40 pages open, 5–10 of which I might still want to read. I need to go through and process that state before I'm happy to close the browser, something I only do about once every week or two. For me, it's the same thing with Microsoft office. I can go a long time without updating the OS for much the same reason.

I'm happy to install patches for things like my todo manager or news reader, both of which always basically show me the same state on startup that I saw on shutdown. The big difference is that if I install the update, my productivity isn't really affected.

My rule of patching is that software vendors should have minimal to no impact on productivity. For instance, don't make me wait, unable to use the application, while I download the updates. Download them in the background, and then only let me know when they're ready to install.

And don't require me to reboot my computer. That should be an absolute last resort. In fact, most operating systems have bent over backward to make sure most programs won't have a legitimate need to do that. Unfortunately, security software is one of those areas where there may still sometimes be a legitimate need.

Of course, it would be great if applications could patch themselves while they're still running, but that's not actually reasonable. However, most software vendors should be able to do a good enough job saving your state that they can shut down, install the updates, then relaunch, restoring your state as if nothing ever happened. All you lose is the minute from when you click "install update" to when you're back up and running.

If productivity impact were minimal, I'd be happy to have most things automatically install updates when I'm idle. For most programs, I don't have the same problem that enterprises have—I don't mind a bit of instability occasionally, as long as the fix is coming soon (or I can easily revert if not).

Either way, people will always be slow to patch, with plenty of people not upgrading their AV (or renewing their expired AV) until they get their next computer. The best thing the industry can do is give people fewer excuses by making sure updates never have a big impact on productivity.

CHAPTER 45

An Open Security Industry

At first blush, it may look like the security industry is pretty open. For example, plenty of companies provide AV by running a ton of AV programs in the cloud and then claiming a program is bad if some number of other AV programs agree that it's bad. Personally, I'm surprised no companies have been sued over such AV "voting" schemes. And while the industry might tolerate this kind of situation, it generally doesn't encourage openness.

There is a tremendous amount of duplication of effort in malware fighting/signature writing across the major vendors. All the companies have dozens of people writing signatures for the same thing. And most of the signatures just amount to simple pattern matching; there's not much intellectual property that's any sort of rocket science. In the meantime, the amount of malware out there is exploding, and no single vendor can grow fast enough to keep up.

While I've argued for a better way of doing things, it is also true that the world would be better off with a standard signature definition language and shared signatures so we're not duplicating effort. This is not as far-fetched as it seems, either. All the major AV vendors already share malware samples with one another on a daily basis. We all get the malware the other guys find. Why duplicate the drudgework?

Instead, let's have the industry compete on the merits of how the players actually do security, and the end user experience. Let's not put unnecessary barriers in the way of becoming as secure as we could possibly be with today's technologies.

Yes, security companies live to make money, but they are also in it to provide the best possible protection to people. Security companies, open your APIs and let everybody integrate. Differentiate yourselves with a product people want to use.

CHAPTER 46

Academics

When I first got into security, I was an academic, writing conference papers, grant proposals, and crap like that. Even in my time consulting and in product development, I have tried to do some things that were both academically interesting and practical.

Having been on both sides of the divide, I'd say that for the most part there is not much practical work coming out of academia that is making a big impact in the real world. There are certainly a few exceptions, most of them in the world of cryptography (that subfield is a lot better with practical applications in general, though there are still a lot of people working on stuff that will never be interesting for real-world systems).

There are lots of reasons for this, an important one being that industry and academia don't share very much. For instance, my first startup built cool security tools for finding bugs, way ahead of what academia was doing. Years later, there are still new papers reinventing things that we did a long time ago but never shared with anybody because we thought we were better off not sharing.

I see the same thing in AV and intrusion detection. Lots of academics are reinventing what industry has been doing for years. Or they're proposing systems that look like they might be viable until someone tries to apply the technique to the real world on a large scale and identifies all the problems (many academic papers on detecting "bad stuff" look good to the authors, but would have serious accuracy problems in the real world).

Academics don't just suffer because they don't know what industry has done. They suffer from not understanding the problems well. Academics don't spend enough time with customers or with companies in the industry to figure out the true problems that need to be solved. Part of this is because academics tend to be more focused on publishable results than on which problems need a better solution.

Academic peer review is a great thing, but in the security field, the fact that publications usually have to meet a high "novelty" bar is a bad thing. The real world would benefit if industry could say, "Here's a proposed system. It's a combination of a lot of ideas, but it's a new, novel system." Right now, academics don't get any credit toward tenure for breaking stuff (though they still might do it for the publicity). But it would be great if academics could get publication credit by publicly analyzing those systems. I think they should get credit for contributing in a practical way to industry—the world would get better systems, after all.

In general, there isn't enough collaboration or communication between academia and industry. Few academics come to the big industry conferences, like RSA (the exceptions are cryptographers). And few people who are building products or are in industry buying security solutions are going to the academic conferences, like IEEE Security and Privacy and USENIX Security. USENIX Security is even supposed to be practically oriented, but when I skim the proceedings, I rarely see anything that really excites me. I can't remember the last time I thought, "That's going to save the world," or even, "Wow, that would save someone some money." On the other hand, I often learn about useful or more cost-effective solutions when talking to people who work in the corporate world.

I don't know how to fix the problem. This is a downward spiral: the less relevant academia is, the less effort industry will put into the relationship, which will leave academia less able to provide value to industry.

Again, even though I think there's a disturbing trend, there are many exceptions. I have a lot of respect for people who are bridging the gap, many of whom I'm proud to call friends (people like Gene Spafford, Avi Rubin, Ed Felten, Tadayoshi Kohno, and David Wagner).

But I'd love to see us do a whole lot better. It pains me to think there are so many smart people out there working hard on security, having so little impact.

CHAPTER 47

Locksmithing

Many offices these days have electronic locks that open with a proximity card. I desperately want these locks for my house, but it's tough to find a regular locksmith who even knows what you're talking about, much less how to install them. Everyone with a clue about this stuff is probably focused on installing it in offices.

Someday this technology will make it to the masses. I hope to have one card for all my locks everywhere. Even better, I'd love to skip the card and use my phone. Plus, let me use some sort of computer-based home-automation system to choose who can use which lock, and when. For example, the kids can get into the liquor cabinet, but only when they turn 40, and only on Christmas Eve.

The lack of locksmiths with technology skills is a big issue today, but it's an issue that time will fix naturally. The biggest problem with the industry is that even the best, most awesome electronic locks need physical keys as backup locks.

It's a fire code thing. What happens if the power goes out in a building and you have to get through a locked door, but the lock is electronic? Either it needs to unlock when the power is out (which is a huge security hole) or you need to have a backup that doesn't require electricity.

Physical locks tend to be really easy to pick unless you go for extremely expensive ones. If it weren't for this pesky power problem, it wouldn't be cost-effective to have a physical lock anywhere we're willing to pay for an electronic lock.

Maybe there's a solution to this conundrum. I think that electronic door locks should all come with a backup power source. Maybe you have to stick an AAA battery into the door and then wave your proximity card. Or maybe the doorknob doubles as a handcrank, and you crank it until there's enough electricity. Certainly, the law should regulate what's acceptable and what's not in order to avoid preventable catastrophes. Nonetheless, we should be able to kill the traditional key-based lock if we really want to do so (though it would take a long time before electronic locks would be anywhere near as cost-effective as physical locks).

Note that many electronic locks use a network to hook into an authentication database. When the power's out, the lock will need either a cached copy of the database or some less regularly updated authentication info in there.

That's not a big deal, though.

CHAPTER 48

Critical Infrastructure

About once a year, there's a big commotion in the security press about attacks on utilities like the power grid. So far, I've never seen any evidence that there have been any significant issues. But that doesn't mean it couldn't happen.

First, it's important to note that the people who design critical infrastructure IT control systems, usually called SCADA systems (Supervisory Control and Data Acquisition), care about these kinds of issues and take them into account when designing. For instance, such systems generally are not ever directly connected to the Internet.

However, there have been several studies showing weaknesses in critical infrastructure systems. I know of several instances in which systems were indirectly accessible from the Internet, despite the intentions of the system designers. For instance, if one computer has two networks, one cable leading to the SCADA system and another to the Internet, anyone on the Internet who breaks in to that machine can see the SCADA system. I have no doubt that there have been many instances in which bad guys have infected a machine that had another foot on a SCADA network, but nobody ever noticed.

What I wonder is how many people are actually looking to target nuclear power plants, the way they do on *24*? Or shut down the Internet (which I've studied for a government project once…it's a heck of a lot harder than you might think)?

Anyway, I am not panicking. I think things are mostly OK. Critical infrastructure has always been most at risk from regular old insider attacks and physical attacks, and I think that's the way it's going to stay, at least until we start hearing about this issue every day for months at a time.

Epilogue

Many people in the security industry like to preach gloom and doom. It makes them money and people usually end up believing what they're selling.

I guess I've been doing the same in this book, preaching gloom and doom. But instead of preaching that the customer is hosed, I'm preaching that the security industry is hosed—I don't think customers are hosed at all. Security issues are, right now, an inconvenience (and in the enterprise, maybe an expensive inconvenience). They aren't a ruinous problem.

When I started working on this book in mid-2008, I'd recently left McAfee to work on a startup. Now, in the last few days of working on this book, I've been brought back into McAfee.

Lots of people have asked me some variation of the question, "Do you feel dirty being back at a big company?" The obvious implication is that they think McAfee sucks (typically, that *all* big companies suck).

Actually, I like McAfee, and am proud of where it is. In the time from when I first started until now, it has essentially gone from middle-of-the-road to best in terms of the quality of its AV solution. Almost all of its security technologies are world-class compared to its competitors. And it's well on its way down the path to implementing some of the grander visions I talk about in this book, such as the move to security in the cloud.

McAfee is phenomenal for meeting enterprise needs, an area that I've tried to avoid as much as possible in this book, but one that is incredibly important to the market.

That is not to say I'm just a McAfee cheerleader. It *is* a big company and there are occasionally things that I don't like. But, I think the leadership is strong, the technology is strong, and the vision is strong, or else I wouldn't be there.

And if I look around the industry, most big companies have positives and negatives. But there is still a massive amount of dysfunction in the industry. Security geeks care about security. They don't worry about usability and they don't worry about cost. The business guys just worry about selling and marketing themselves to make it easier to sell, even if they arm the bad guys in the process.

Customers may think they need security, but they usually don't want it. And, when they have it, the experience often sucks. It's not always clear that they're better off paying for security.

On the whole, I'm disappointed in where we are, even though I understand why we're here. I think it wouldn't be hard to do better. In some cases, industry is on the path, just not moving quickly at all.

Real, timely improvement is possible, but it requires people to care a lot more than they do. I'm not sure that's going to happen anytime soon. But I hope it does.

Index

About the Author

John Viega is CTO of the Software-as-a-Service Business Unit at McAfee, and was previously Vice President, Chief Security Architect at McAfee. He is an active advisor to several security companies, including Fortify and Bit9. He is the author of a number of security books, including *Network Security with OpenSSL* (O'Reilly) and *Building Secure Software* (Addison-Wesley), and is co-editor of O'Reilly's *Beautiful Security*.

John is responsible for numerous software security tools and is the original author of Mailman, the popular mailing list manager. He has done extensive standards work in the IEEE and IETF, and co-invented GCM, a cryptographic algorithm that NIST (U.S. Department of Commerce) has standardized. He holds a B.A. and M.S. from the University of Virginia.

Colophon

The cover image is a stock photo from Jupiter Images. The cover fonts are BentonSans and Sabon. The text font is Sabon; the heading font is BentonSans.

Related Titles from O'Reilly

Security

802.11 Security

Apache Security

Building Internet Firewalls, *2nd Edition*

Computer Security Basics, *2nd Edition*

Digital Identity

Hardening Cisco Routers

Internet Forensics

Kerberos: The Definitive Guide

Linux Security Cookbook

Managing Security with Snort and IDS Tools

Mastering FreeBSD OpenBSD Security

Network Security Assessment , *2nd Edition*

Network Security Hacks, *2nd Edition*

Network Security with OpenSSL

Network Security Tools

Network Warrior

Practical Unix and Internet Security, *3rd Edition*

Programming .NET Security

RADIUS

Secure Coding: Principles and Practices

Secure Programming Cookbook for C and C++

Security and Usability

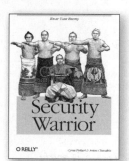

Security Power Tools

Security Warrior

SSH, The Secure Shell: The Definitive Guide, *2nd Edition*

Snort Cookbook

SpamAssassin

Web Security, Privacy and Commerce, *2nd Edition*

Windows Server 2003 Security Cookbook

Try the online edition free for 45 days

the myths of security

the ultimate insiders guide to network security

john viega

O'REILLY®

Get the information you need when you need it, with Safari Books Online. Safari Books Online contains the complete version of the print book in your hands plus thousands of titles from the best technical publishers, with sample code ready to cut and paste into your applications.

Safari is designed for people in a hurry to get the answers they need so they can get the job done. You can find what you need in the morning, and put it to work in the afternoon. As simple as cut, paste, and program.

To try out Safari and the online edition of the above title FREE for 45 days, go to www.oreilly.com/go/safarienabled and enter the coupon code FDOZGAA.

To see the complete Safari Library visit:
safari.oreilly.com

Safari.
Books Online